The Concerto
Parts I–III
Robert Greenberg, Ph.D.

PUBLISHED BY:

THE TEACHING COMPANY
4151 Lafayette Center Drive, Suite 100
Chantilly, Virginia 20151-1232
1-800-TEACH-12
Fax—703-378-3819
www.teach12.com

Copyright © The Teaching Company, 2006

Printed in the United States of America

This book is in copyright. All rights reserved.

Without limiting the rights under copyright reserved above,
no part of this publication may be reproduced, stored in
or introduced into a retrieval system, or transmitted,
in any form, or by any means
(electronic, mechanical, photocopying, recording, or otherwise),
without the prior written permission of
The Teaching Company.

Robert Greenberg, Ph.D.

San Francisco Performances

Robert Greenberg was born in Brooklyn, New York, in 1954 and has lived in the San Francisco Bay area since 1978. He received a B.A. in music, magna cum laude, from Princeton University in 1976 where his principal teachers were Edward Cone, Daniel Werts, and Carlton Gamer in composition; Claudio Spies and Paul Lansky in analysis; and Jerry Kuderna in piano. In 1984, he received a Ph.D. in music composition, with distinction, from the University of California, Berkeley, where his principal teachers were Andrew Imbrie and Olly Wilson in composition and Richard Felciano in analysis.

He has composed over 45 works for a wide variety of instrumental and vocal ensembles. His works have been performed in New York, San Francisco, Chicago, Los Angeles, England, Ireland, Greece, Italy, and the Netherlands, where the Amsterdam Concertgebouw performed his *Child's Play* for String Quartet. He has received numerous honors, including three Nicola de Lorenzo Composition Prizes and three Meet-the-Composer Grants. Recent commissions have come from the Koussevitzky Foundation at the Library of Congress, the Alexander String Quartet, the San Francisco Contemporary Music Players, San Francisco Performances, the Strata Ensemble, and the XTET ensemble.

Professor Greenberg is a board member and an artistic director of COMPOSERS, INC., a composers' collective/production organization based in San Francisco. His music is published by Fallen Leaf Press and CPP/Belwin and is recorded on the Innova label. He has performed, taught, and lectured extensively across North America and Europe. He is currently music-historian-in-residence with San Francisco Performances, where he has lectured and performed since 1994, and resident composer and music historian to National Public Radio's "Weekend All Things Considered." He has served on the faculties of the University of California at Berkeley, California State University at Hayward, and the San Francisco Conservatory of Music, where he chaired the Department of Music, History and Literature from 1989–2001 and served as the Director of the Adult Extension Division from 1991–1996.

Professor Greenberg has lectured for some of the most prestigious musical and arts organizations in the United States, including the San Francisco Symphony (where, for 10 years, he was host and lecturer for the symphony's nationally acclaimed "Discovery Series"), the Lincoln Center for the Performing Arts, the Van Cliburn Foundation, and the Chautauqua Institute. He is a sought-after lecturer for businesses and business schools, speaking at such diverse organizations as the Commonwealth Club of San Francisco and the University of Chicago Graduate School of Business, and has been profiled in various major publications, including the *Wall Street Journal*, *Inc.* magazine, and the London *Times*.

Table of Contents
The Concerto

Professor Biography i
Course Scope 1
Lecture One   The Voice in the Wilderness 5
Lecture Two   The Baroque Italian Concerto 11
Lecture Three   Baroque Masters 17
Lecture Four   Bach's *Brandenburg* Concerti 24
Lecture Five   Mozart, Part 1 31
Lecture Six   Mozart, Part 2 39
Lecture Seven   Classical Masters 45
Lecture Eight   Beethoven 51
Lecture Nine   The Romantic Concerto 58
Lecture Ten   Hummel and Chopin 65
Lecture Eleven   Mendelssohn and Schumann 72
Lecture Twelve   Romantic Masters 79
Lecture Thirteen   Tchaikovsky 86
Lecture Fourteen   Brahms and the Symphonic Concerto 93
Lecture Fifteen   Dvorak 102
Lecture Sixteen   Rachmaninoff 110
Lecture Seventeen   The Russian Concerto, Part 1 118
Lecture Eighteen   The Russian Concerto, Part 2 124
Lecture Nineteen   The Concerto in France 131
Lecture Twenty   Bartok 139
Lecture Twenty-One   Schönberg, Berg and the 12-Tone Method 146
Lecture Twenty-Two   Twentieth-Century Masters 155
Lecture Twenty-Three   Elliott Carter 163
Lecture Twenty-Four   Servants to the Cause and Guilty Pleasures ... 170
Timeline 175
Glossary 181
Featured Composers 190
Bibliography 193

The Concerto

Scope:

There is no doubt about it: The concerto has all the blood, sweat, tears, and triumph of the opera house from which it was born! It is, at its core, a theatrical construct. Ringing forth against the mass of the orchestra, the individual solo voice (or voices) is a metaphor for the empowered individual reveling in his individuality. This relationship between the soloist and the orchestra gives the concerto an extra dimension that underlines its theatricality—it is as much about the performers as about the music itself. The various relationships between soloist and orchestra, embodied collectively in the concerto repertoire, demonstrate almost every human relationship we can imagine, from the most tender to the most confrontational. On top of this, the relationship between the soloist herself and her instrument represents life lived at the edge, as the concerto genre affords the composer an opportunity to explore the extreme capabilities of solo performers.

Our own explorations of the concerto will reveal a huge repertoire, dating all the way back to the late 1600s, when the genre was invented. We will survey the concerto's history from its conception as a child of Renaissance ideals through the 20th century, and as we go, we will observe this genre's metamorphosis and the degree to which its development reflected changing social and artistic environments. We will also observe the concerto's evolving theatricality, which as we will see, increasingly becomes a metaphor for the individual and the collective.

The concerto's evolution began in Italy in the late 1500s, when homogenous musical textures were being replaced with music that explored the idea of contrast. In the polychoral music of such Venetian composers as Giovanni Gabrieli, we hear the first great flowering of the *concerto principle*, or *concertato style*—music that explores the concepts of contrast and even conflict. By the turn of the 17th century, the Humanism of the Renaissance and its celebration of individualism had inspired the invention of opera: The concept of *tune* evolved; new harmonies evolved to accompany singers; the orchestra was born; and opera's dramatic essence required that composers experiment with emotionally expressive musical materials. By the 1680s, opera's influence—its melodic, harmonic, structural, and expressive elements—had found its way into instrumental compositions, and the first true concerti began to appear, including those of Arcangelo Corelli (1653–1713), who laid the genre's foundation. Corelli wrote a type of concerto known as a *concerto grosso*: Instead of one soloist, this genre had a small group of soloists, called the *concertino*, which was contrasted with the main instrumental ensemble, called the *grosso*. The concerto grosso was brought to its full flowering in the High Baroque by Italian and German composers, including the greatest master of them all, Johann Sebastian Bach (1685–1750), whose concerti had no equal until those of Mozart.

Alongside the development of the concerto grosso was that of the solo concerto. It first appeared as a result of the use of the solo trumpet in Bolognese civic traditions, and its development owed a great deal to the perfection and cult of the violin in the 17th century. Antonio Vivaldi (1678–1741) expanded the expressive capabilities of the violin and made the concerto the most important type of instrumental music during the High Baroque. By this time, a three-movement structure had been established for the concerto (fast–slow–fast), while the contrast between soloist and the main ensemble (also known as the grosso or the *ripieno*) became much more pronounced and the soloist's material, more virtuosic. The violin was typically the solo "star" of the High Baroque Italian concerto, although many concerti were written for wind and brass instruments.

Thanks in large part to music publishers based in Amsterdam, the Italian concerto became known in northern Europe, where it quickly became a favorite genre of composition. Such German-speaking composers as Telemann, Handel, and J. S. Bach brought the concerto to a new level of sophistication and compositional complexity that far exceeded their Italian models.

By the mid-18th century, the Enlightenment era was in full bloom, and its doctrine of accessibility— what is good for the greatest number is what is best—was translated into a musical aesthetic that defined the best music as music that appealed to the greatest number of listeners. Importantly, it was understood that such music would be well crafted and in "good taste." In practice, this put the focus on clarity and balance—clarity of phrase structures and clear, carefully balanced formal structures—beautiful melodies, and expressive restraint. The emphasis on clear, vocally conceived melody necessitated the creation of more flexible forms that could accommodate multiple themes and stressed, far more than before, thematic contrast and departure and return. Among the formal structures from the new musical aesthetic of the Enlightenment (or what is now called the Classical era) are sonata (or sonata allegro) form and double-exposition form, a version of sonata form specifically geared to the concerto genre. The solo concerto became the predominant concerto type in the Classical era, and concerti for keyboard (harpsichord and piano) began to replace the violin as the favored solo instrument. The single Classical-era composer who brought all these elements together in one dazzling and transcendental body of concerti was Wolfgang Mozart (1756–1791). In Mozart's concerti, we will also see how the relationship between soloist and orchestra emphasizes collaboration. The potential conflicts of concertato style are almost foreign to Mozart's compositional style.

The same cannot be said of the concerti of Ludwig van Beethoven (1770–1827), who saw the world in terms of conflict and catharsis. With Beethoven, the concerto became a metaphor, to a greater degree than ever before, for the individual (the soloist) struggling against the collective (the orchestra). Beethoven's belief that expressive content should be given free rein to determine form manifested itself in an expressive content and formal flexibility that often shocked and even dismayed his audiences. With Beethoven, too, comes a concept of the solo piano as an orchestra unto itself. His writing for the piano was very different from Mozart's, and the kind of power that he sought from the instrument would not be completely realized until the modern piano emerged in the 1830s and 1840s.

In many ways, Beethoven both anticipated and inspired the 19th-century aesthetic philosophy known as Romanticism. His view of the artist as hero, represented in the concerto genre by the soloist, was expanded in the virtuoso Romantic concerto to the point that a genuine partnership between the soloist and orchestra became impossible. The Romantic soloist dominates the musical scene, and technical prowess becomes *de rigueur*. By the time the glittering concerti of Franz Liszt (1811–1886) arrive on the scene, the role of the orchestra is so reduced that double-exposition form no longer has any relevancy to a genre that has come to worship the virtuoso soloist as a god. But there were exceptions in the over-the-top world of the Romantic concerto. Felix Mendelssohn (1809–1847), Robert Schumann (1810–1856), and particularly Johannes Brahms (1833—1897) wrote concerti that treat the soloist and orchestra as equal partners and avoid the use of virtuosity for its own sake. The late-19th- and early-20th-century concerto was also a receptacle for another aspect of Romanticism—nationalism. Folk music inspired concerto composers across Europe and

Russia, such as the Bohemian master Antonin Dvorak (1841–1904), the Russian-born cosmopolitan Sergei Rachmaninoff (1873–1943), and the Hungarian Bela Bartok (1881–1945).

As the concerto makes its way through the first decades of the 20th century, it comes under the influence of American jazz, while in France, Impressionism makes itself felt musically in the genre. Sonority becomes as important an element in the French concerto as melody, harmony, and rhythm; thematic variation becomes at least as important as thematic development. Those same years heard sound take a revolutionary turn in the music of Arnold Schönberg (1874–1951), who developed a system to liberate melody from what he considered to be the bondage of traditional harmony. His 12-tone method of composition broke with the centuries-old system of consonant/dissonant, major/minor harmonies and opened the door to an entirely new world of musical expression, in which polyphony was of central importance. The essence of polyphony—the interplay of multiple simultaneous melodies—was stretched to a new "mega" level in the groundbreaking music of Elliott Carter (b. 1908), whose great achievement was to simultaneously layer multiple, completely different musical elements in a convincingly homogenous whole. In doing so, he evoked the democratic ideal that celebrates the uniqueness of the individual voice and recognizes its responsibility to contribute to a whole greater than itself. The concerto genre, always responsive to innovation, has been enriched by the polyphonic revolutions of both Schönberg and Carter.

Perhaps more than any other orchestral genre, the concerto grew directly out of vocal music and vocal compositional models; its roots in opera make it a genuinely theatrical construct that became a metaphor for the individual, sometimes in conflict and sometimes in collaboration with the collective. Many superb concerti are introduced in this course; many more remain to be explored in this singularly exciting genre that continues to attract new generations of composers and to endow listeners with rich rewards.

Note: Dr. Greenberg begs the indulgence of the Teaching Company community in his use of the Italian plural "concerti," as he has found himself, after decades of ingrained habit, incapable of using the anglicized plural, "concertos."

Lecture One
The Voice in the Wilderness

Scope: The secularization and Humanism of the late 16th and 17th centuries led to the flowering of the *concerto principle*, as seen in the polychoral works of such composers as Giovanni Gabrieli, and to the invention of opera. Both developments would contribute directly to the evolution of the concerto. Alessandro Stradella was the first composer to write works that we accept today as concerti. His Sonata in D Major for Trumpet and Strings (c. 1680) is really a concerto, exemplifying, as it does, the idea of contrast and contest—the *concerto principle*. In this work, we see, for the first time, how an operatic technique is transferred to instrumental music. The solo singer (here, the trumpet) is accompanied by two string ensembles, a small group (*concertino*) and a larger group (*grosso*), which contrast and contest with each other. This type of concerto, with two contrasting instrumental groups, became known as the *concerto grosso*. Arcangelo Corelli's concerti grossi provided the foundation of the concerto genre. Many of these works were written circa 1682 and became the most influential orchestral works composed in the 17th century, with their marvelous use of the concerto principle.

Outline

I. The genre of the concerto has all the dramatic force of the opera house: It features a solo voice or voices against the mass of the orchestra, and the concerto repertoire embodies almost every human relationship imaginable, from the most tender to the most violent. Performance of a concerto represents life lived at the edge, as the solo instruments and the musicians who play them are often pushed to the limit of practicable possibilities.

   A. Because of the "singularity" of the soloist's voice, the range and immediacy of expression inherent in the concerto exceeds that of every other type of music, except opera (which gave birth to the concerto during the late 17th century, as we will see). Where the symphony (another genre birthed by opera) evolved toward abstraction, the concerto never lost its essentially theatrical roots.

- **B.** Given that the concerto was invented well over 300 years ago, its repertoire is huge. During the 18th and 19th centuries, at least as many concerti were written as symphonies, and during the 20th century, the concerto was, by far, the single most important genre of orchestral music.
- **C.** **Musical selections:** Vivaldi, "Spring" from *The Four Seasons*, movement 1, opening (1725); Johann Sebastian Bach, *Brandenburg* Concerto no. 2, movement 3, opening (c. 1721); Mozart, Piano Concerto no. 21 in C Major, K. 467, movement 2 (1785); Liszt, Piano Concerto in Eb Major, movement 1 (1853); Bartok, Concerto for Orchestra, movement 5, opening (1943); Carter, Double Concerto for Harpsichord and Piano, A*llegro scherzando* (1961).

II. The genre is based on relationships. It is as much about relationships between the performers themselves as it is about the music performed.
- **A.** While a symphony is about its themes—how they are contrasted, varied, transformed, developed, and so forth—a concerto adds an extra dimension: a soloist or group of soloists.
- **B.** This adds a theatrical element to the mix. We see a *person*, not just an instrument. The concerto is as much about the individual (the soloist) versus the collective (the orchestra) as the music performed.

III. This course has three goals:
- **A.** To survey the history of the concerto from its invention in Italy in the late 1600s through the 20th century.
- **B.** To explore the evolving nature of the concerto genre and the degree to which that evolution is a reflection of a changing social and artistic environment.
- **C.** To observe the evolving theatricality of the concerto and the degree to which this theatricality is a metaphor for the individual and the collective.

IV. The word *concerto* comes from the Italian verb *concertare*, meaning "to join together" and "to be in agreement with." The earliest surviving music score bearing the name *concerto* was printed in Venice in 1587—a series of compositions by Andrea and Giovanni Gabrieli entitled *Concerti per voci e stromenti musicali* ("Concerti for Voices and Musical Instruments").

- **A.** The past participle of the word *concerto* is *concertato*. It developed a different musical meaning: "to fight" or "to contest with."
- **B.** The growing secularization and Humanism of the late 16th and 17th centuries had a significant impact on the music of that time. The homogenous musical textures of the early 16th century were, by the late 17th century, being replaced by bold contrasts of sound.
- **C.** The first great flowering of the *concerto principle*—the *concertato style*—was centered in St. Mark's Cathedral in Venice during the late 1500s. The fact that St. Mark's has two widely spaced organ lofts encouraged composers to experiment by placing instrumental and vocal choirs in different locations. The resultant *polychoral* music is all about bold effect.
- **D.** An example is Giovanni Gabrieli's *Buccinate in neomenia tuba* ("Blow the Trumpet in the New Moon," c. 1600). It is scored for four different choirs, totaling 19 different instrumental and voice parts! Let's be aware of bold contrasts between instrumental and vocal sonorities, as the choirs alternate with each other and play together in various combinations. **Musical selection:** Gabrieli, *Buccinate in neomenia tuba.*

V. The same Renaissance-inspired, Humanistic expressive impulse that led to the creation of the polychoral works of Gabrieli also brought about the invention of opera, in Florence, during the last years of the 16th century.

- **A.** Opera celebrated the primacy of individual emotion, and a new musical vocabulary evolved to accommodate the expressive needs of the operatic stage.
- **B.** The concept of *tune* evolved.
- **C.** A new sort of harmonic accompaniment was invented to accompany singers, which came to be known as *basso continuo* and became ubiquitous in the vocal and instrumental music of the Baroque.
- **D.** Larger instrumental ensembles evolved—the orchestra was born.

- **E.** The dramatic situations that opera depicted forced composers to experiment with emotionally expressive musical materials.
- **F.** Opera created the concept of a musical "first man" and "first woman"—the "stars" of the performance.
- **G.** All these operatic developments contributed to the invention of the concerto.

VI. The invention of the violin was also important to the development of the concerto.
- **A.** The violin family of instruments (violin, viola, and 'cello) began to emerge from workshops in northern Italy between 1520 and 1530. Over the next 200 years, the violin family was brought to perfection by a series of master luthiers working out of Cremona. They included Nicolo Amati, Andrea Guarneri, Francesco Rugeri, and Antonio Stradiveri.
- **B.** The "star" of the violin family was, and still is, the violin. Its rise as the principal instrument in Western music corresponded with the rise of opera.
- **C.** The 17th-century cult of the violin preconditioned composers to think operatically in their instrumental music.
- **D.** The great Italian Baroque composers of concerti were violinists by training.

VII. The first composer to write what we accept today as concerti was Alessandro Stradella (1644–1682).
- **A.** Stradella's concerti are concerti grossi, which contrast two ensembles: a small group of solo instruments and a full string section. The small solo group is called a *concertino*, while the string orchestra is called the *grosso*, or the *ripieno*.
- **B.** Stradella cut his musical teeth composing operas, for which he developed a style of vocal accompaniment that alternated a small group of strings with the full string ensemble. This technique found its way directly into his purely instrumental Sonata in D Major for Trumpet and Strings (c. 1680).
- **C.** Despite its title, this piece really is a concerto grosso with the addition of a solo trumpet that mediates between the two string ensembles.

    D. What makes this a concerto is not just the solo trumpet but the nature of the accompaniment, comprising a small ensemble (concertino) and large ensemble (grosso or ripieno). These two ensembles contend and contrast with each other, and thus, the piece is in the concertato style. **Musical selection:** Stradella, Sonata in D Major for Trumpet and Strings, movement 1.

VIII. Arcangelo Corelli (1653–1713) created a body of printed music that was performed, studied, and imitated for more than 50 years. His published works consist entirely of instrumental music.

    A. Corelli's Twelve Concerti Grossi, op. 6, were published in 1714, and the majority of them were most probably written around 1682, making them among the earliest concerti composed. They are scored for string orchestra and basso continuo. The concertino consists of two violins and a 'cello.

    B. The contrast is not so much thematic as it is instrumental.

    C. The Concerto no. 8 in G Minor (*Christmas*) is in six movements. The first opens with an introductory phrase for both the concertino and the grosso (*tutti*); then, the concertino instruments enter one at a time; and finally, the grosso enters. **Musical selection:** Corelli, Concerto Grosso in G Minor, op. 6, no. 8, movement 1 (1690).

    D. The second movement, marked *allegro* ("fast"), puts the concertino at the forefront. **Musical selection:** Corelli, Concerto Grosso in G Minor, op. 6, no. 8, movement 2.

    E. The slow third-movement opening sees each new phrase initiated by the concertino and concluded by the tutti. **Musical selection:** Corelli, Concerto Grosso in G Minor, op. 6, no. 8, movement 3.

    F. The fourth movement, marked *vivace* ("lively"), is a dance-like movement in which the concertino and tutti alternate, phrase by phrase. **Musical selection:** Corelli, Concerto Grosso in G Minor, op. 6, no. 8, movement 4.

    G. The brilliant fifth movement is the most directly concertato-style movement in the piece. **Musical selection:** Corelli, Concerto Grosso in G Minor, op. 6, no. 8, movement 5.

    H. The sixth and final movement is the single longest movement in any of Corelli's published concerti. It is marked *Pastorale*, and its rustic character is provided by the simple, almost folk-like melody and the bagpipe-like drone in the accompaniment. In this

movement, which makes a distinct contrast with the preceding movement, the concertino and tutti alternate in collaboration.
Musical selection: Corelli, Concerto Grosso in G Minor, op. 6, no. 8, movement 6.

I. Corelli's concerti grossi represent the Italian mid-Baroque at its very best.

Lecture Two
The Baroque Italian Concerto

Scope: The large-scale orchestral compositions that began to emerge in the 1660s and 1670s were inspired equally by the opera house and the recently perfected violin. They employed the concertato style as their compositional basis. Alongside the development of the concerto grosso was that of the solo concerto. This type of concerto initially grew out of the civic traditions of Bologna, Italy, where trumpet players had honed incredible skills playing valveless trumpets, inspiring composers to write concerti for the instrument. Two important contributions to the development of the concerto were made by Giuseppe Torelli, the most famous of the Bolognese composers. Inspired by operatic practices, Torelli gave his concerti three distinct movements, a scheme that remained the rule through the 20th century, and he invented *ritornello* form. In 17th-century Venice, music flourished as never before. Tomaso Albinoni elevated the solo oboe to a position almost equal to that of the solo violin, while Antonio Vivaldi expanded the expressive capabilities of the violin and made the concerto the most important type of instrumental music during the High Baroque.

Outline

I. Even as Corelli was developing the concerto grosso in Rome, other composers in Bologna were creating what would become the solo concerto.

   A. The solo concerto features one soloist, rather than the group of soloists characteristic of the concerto grosso.

   B. The first solo concerti were written for trumpet and strings. They evolved out of the traditional use of the trumpet in Bologna for civic occasions.

   C. The type of trumpet used in 17th-century Bologna was a valveless horn, used primarily in its high (*clarino*) register and limited to passages that outlined simple harmonies or featured scales. The huge physical strain these trumpets exerted on their players necessitated frequent breaks. This meant that composers had to shift constantly between the trumpet and the strings, reinforcing the effect of the concertato-style writing.

II. Giuseppe Torelli's Concerto in D Major for Trumpet and Strings (c. 1695) is an example of the Bolognese trumpet concerto at its zenith.

   A. Torelli (1658–1709) was the most famous of all the Bolognese composers and the most prolific. His trumpet concerti were inspired by a particular performer, as will so often be the case for concerti composers. In Torelli's case, the performer was Giovanni Pellegrino Brandi.

   B. An important innovation that Torelli introduced in his solo concerti was inspired by operatic practice; he modeled his concerti on Italian opera overtures, which were typically structured in three parts: fast–slow–fast. This innovation remained the rule for concerti through the 20th century.

   C. The first movement of Torelli's Concerto in D Major for Trumpet and Strings opens with an upbeat, graceful theme, scored for the string ensemble (grosso or ripieno). **Musical selection:** Torelli, Concerto in D Major for Trumpet and Strings, movement 1, opening theme.

   D. The opening of this theme is immediately repeated by the solo trumpet, after which, the ripieno and trumpet trade phrases back and forth with each other. **Musical selection:** Torelli, Concerto in D Major for Trumpet and Strings, movement 1.

   E. The remainder of the movement consists of a free working-out of melodic fragments drawn from the theme. The trumpet and ripieno (string ensemble) alternate constantly, sometimes repeating each other's material, sometimes presenting different material; sometimes one accompanies the other, and sometimes one drops out completely. It is a perfect example of the concertato style. **Musical selection:** Torelli, Concerto in D Major for Trumpet and Strings, movement 1, remainder.

   F. The second movement is in three-part form (A–B–C). The opening and closing sections (A) are slow and the middle section (B) is fast.

      1. It is typical of Torelli's trumpet concerti that the trumpet takes a break in this middle movement. But even without the trumpet, this movement acts like a concerto within a concerto.

The opening A section is played by the entire string ensemble. **Musical selection:** Torelli, Concerto in D Major for Trumpet and Strings, movement 2, opening.
2. The fast middle section (B) features two alternating solo violins heard against the rest of the ensemble—a miniature concerto grosso! **Musical selection:** Torelli, Concerto in D Major for Trumpet and Strings, movement 2, B.
3. When the slow music returns in the concluding section of the movement, a solo violin takes the lead, creating the effect of a solo concerto for violin! **Musical selection:** Torelli, Concerto in D Major for Trumpet and Strings, movement 2, A^1.

G. The solo trumpet re-enters for the third and final movement. **Musical selection:** Torelli, Concerto in D Major for Trumpet and Strings, movement 3, opening.

H. In addition to his three-movement scheme, Torelli made another lasting contribution to the development of the concerto, inspired by the operatic aria.
1. In the opera arias of Torelli's day, the voice was typically accompanied as simply as possible by the basso continuo—a "mini" ensemble consisting, usually, of a harpsichord and a 'cello. Between the aria verses, the full orchestra would enter and play its own material like a refrain, a passage called a *ritornello*.
2. Torelli experimented with such ritornello techniques in his concerti, especially the first movements.

III. Thanks to Corelli and Torelli, the next generation of composers, centered in Venice, built on instrumental as well as vocal models.

A. Venetian music flourished in the 17th century, especially in the city's orphanages for abandoned girls, who enjoyed a high standard of musical education. Many students became virtuosi and inspired the creation of a tremendous amount of instrumental music.

B. The concerto became the instrumental equivalent of opera and developed distinctive features:
1. A three-movement scheme (fast–slow–fast).
2. Use of the ritornello form in the first and, occasionally, in the second and third movements.

3. Relatively simple and catchy ritornello themes, played by the ensembles.
4. Contrasting and virtuosic material, played by the soloist.
5. Slow movements that are genuinely operatic in their lyricism and expressive content.

IV. The Venetian composer Tomaso Albinoni (1671–1751) wrote a great deal of music, including 59 concerti. His Concerto in D Minor for Oboe and Strings, op. 9, no. 2, reflects the Venetian tendency to compose concerti for woodwinds as well as strings. Concerti for oboe, however, were rare at that time. Albinoni's interest in the oboe came from his interest in the human voice—he was a singing coach and his wife was an opera singer.

  A. In the first movement of Albinoni's D Minor Oboe Concerto (c. 1722), the oboe and the ripieno take turns stating the ritornello theme. **Musical selection:** Albinoni, Concerto in D Minor for Oboe and Strings, op. 9, no. 2, movement 1, ritornello theme.

  B. The oboe enters with an abbreviated version of the theme, punctuated by the ripieno. All of this is freely repeated. **Musical selection:** Albinoni, Concerto in D Minor for Oboe and Strings, op. 9, no. 2, movement 1. From this point of the movement on, the ripieno plays the ritornelli and the oboe plays new, contrasting episodes.

  C. The second movement (*adagio*) begins with an orchestral introduction that anticipates the utterly vocal oboe theme that follows. **Musical selection:** Albinoni, Concerto in D Minor for Oboe and Strings, op. 9, no. 2, movement 2.

  D. The third-movement ritornello form is built like the first movement: The ritornello theme is stated first by the ripieno, then by the solo oboe. **Musical selection:** Albinoni, Concerto in D Minor for Oboe and Strings, op. 9, no. 2, movement 3.

  E. From this point in the movement, the oboe plays a series of increasingly virtuosic episodes, punctuated by the ripieno. When the ritornello theme returns in its entirety at the very end of the movement, it is played by the oboe. **Musical selection:** Albinoni, Concerto in D Minor for Oboe and Strings, op. 9, no. 2, movement 3, remainder.

V. The most well known of Venice's four orphanages/conservatories was the Pieta. By 1700, it was the best school of music in northern Italy. The students played and sang for chapel services and gave concerts when the theater season was over. For 37 years, the violin master, conductor, composer, and sometime general superintendent of music at the Pieta was a priest named Antonio Lucio Vivaldi.

    A. Vivaldi (1678–1741), nicknamed the Red Priest for his red hair, was a virtuoso violinist. He is best known for his concerti—he composed more than 500 of them. About half are for solo violin and orchestra, and virtually all were written for performance at the Pieta.

    B. Vivaldi composed concerti for all sorts of instrumental combinations and in a variety of concerto forms: solo concerti, concerti grossi, and ripieno concerti. Vivaldi's compositional style exhibits three characteristics:

        1. In large-scale structure and form, Vivaldi's concerti are not innovative: They are almost always in three movements, follow the conventional fast–slow–fast scheme, and are almost invariably cast in ritornello form.

        2. What distinguishes his concerti from those of his models are the complexity of his themes, the degree of contrast between the ripieno and the soloists, the virtuosity of his solo parts, and the large-scale dramatic flow and length of his movements.

        3. It is in his violin writing that Vivaldi *does* become an innovator: his use of arpeggios, the upper register of the violin, bowing, and articulation and his ability to make the violin sound like things other than a violin.

    C. Vivaldi's thee-movement violin concerti known as *The Four Seasons* are among the best known concerti in the repertoire. Each concerto is based on a sonnet extolling the merits of a particular season.

        1. The first of the concerti, the Concerto in E Major for Violin, op. 8, no. 1, subtitled "Spring," was composed between 1718 and 1720 and published in 1725. It is based on a sonnet by an unknown author:

> Spring has arrived, and merrily
> The birds hail her with happy song.
> And, meanwhile, at the breath of the Zephyrs,

> The streams flow with a sweet murmur.
>
> Thunder and lightning, chosen to proclaim her,
> Come covering the sky with a black mantle.
> And then, when these fall silent, the little birds
> Return once more to their melodious incantation.

    2. The first movement is in ritornello form. **Musical selection:** Vivaldi, *The Four Seasons*, "Spring," movement 1, opening ritornello.

    3. The soloist illustrates the details of the sonnet. The first contrasting episode corresponds to the sonnet's line: "and merrily the birds hail spring with happy song." **Musical selection:** Vivaldi, *The Four Seasons*, "Spring," movement 1, first contrasting episode and abbreviated (tutti) return to the ritornello theme.

    4. The next passage (tutti) corresponds to the lines: "And, meanwhile, at the breath of the Zephyrs, the streams flow with a sweet murmur." **Musical selection:** Vivaldi, *The Four Seasons*, "Spring," movement 1.

    5. The lightning and rain are depicted by virtuosic arpeggios in the solo violin, while the ripieno represents the thunder, followed by a return, in the minor, to the ritornello theme. **Musical selection:** Vivaldi, *The Four Seasons*, "Spring," movement 1.

    6. The storm ends and the "little birds return once more…" The movement concludes with a last appearance of the ritornello theme. **Musical selection:** Vivaldi, *The Four Seasons*, "Spring," movement 1, remainder.

D. Vivaldi's Violin Concerto in Eb Major, op. 8, no. 5 (c. 1720), is nicknamed *La Tempesta di mare* ("The Storm at Sea"). The real storm is the incredibly virtuosic writing for the solo violin. **Musical selection:** Violin Concerto in Eb Major, op. 8, no. 5, movement 1, opening.

E. Vivaldi, who enjoyed fame and fortune in his lifetime, died a poor man in Vienna. He refined and intensified the concerto and almost single-handedly elevated the genre to the most important type of instrumental music during the High Baroque. His concerti, along with those of Corelli, became the ground-line standard for the next generation of concerto composers.

Lecture Three
Baroque Masters

Scope: Among the most notable of Baroque composers was Alessandro Marcello, best known for his consummately crafted concerti. His D Minor Oboe Concerto, which inspired Johann Sebastian Bach to arrange it for harpsichord, is rich in expressive depth and brilliant virtuosic writing. In his concerti grossi, Francesco Geminiani masterfully combined the conservative model of Corelli with the contemporary trends of virtuosic writing and counterpoint. Francesco Manfredini, as a student of Torelli, could observe and extend that master's development of the solo concerto. Pietro Locatelli's wildly expressive concerti, unappreciated by many of his contemporaries, are quite different from any of the Baroque concerti so far discussed. Georg Muffat was the first significant composer of concerti who was not an Italian. His Concerto Grosso no. 5 in D Major is a wonderful hybrid of the French and Italian styles of his day. An eclectic approach to music is also taken by the next two composers. Georg Philipp Telemann's music represents a fusion of Italian and French musical genres and styles with German intensity of expression and emphasis on technique. In his concerti grossi, George Frederick Handel masterfully fused old and new, along with a diversity of elements that give the whole a truly cosmopolitan flavor.

Outline

I. Alessandro Marcello (1684–1750) was one of the most important composers of concerti of his day. As a nobleman, he did not have to compose for a living but did so for the pleasure of it. And he was a consummate craftsman.

   A. Marcello's most well known concerto is the Oboe Concerto in D Minor, published circa 1718.

   B. The first-movement ritornello form opens with a theme of great expressive depth. We hear the concerto in a version transcribed for trumpet. **Musical selection:** Marcello, Oboe (transcribed for trumpet) Concerto in C Minor, movement 1, ritornello theme and first solo.

- **C.** The second movement is a gorgeous aria for soloist and orchestra. **Musical selection:** Marcello, Oboe (transcribed for trumpet) Concerto in C Minor, movement 2.
- **D.** The third-movement finale is a virtuosic tour-de-force, in which the ripieno comments on and echoes phrases initially played by the soloist. **Musical selection:** Marcello, Oboe (transcribed for trumpet) Concerto in C Minor, movement 3.
- **E.** Johann Sebastian Bach arranged Marcello's Oboe Concerto in D Minor for harpsichord. Let's compare the two versions. **Musical selection:** Marcello, Oboe (transcribed for trumpet) Concerto in C Minor, movement 3; Bach, Harpsichord Concerto in D Minor, BWV 974.
- **F.** The English musicologist Arthur Hutchings described Marcello's concerto as "one of the supremely beautiful works of the Venetian school."

II. Francesco Geminiani (1687–1762), who studied under Corelli, lived and worked in England and Ireland most of his life.
- **A.** Geminiani's concerti are clearly modeled on those of Corelli.
- **B.** Most of them are concerti grossi.
- **C.** Many of them employ Corelli's trademark concertino—two violins and a 'cello.
- **D.** Geminiani also used Corelli's older, four-movement scheme, rather than the three-movement scheme.
- **E.** Geminiani was, however, completely "modern" in the degree of virtuosity that he demanded and in his extraordinary skills as a contrapuntalist (a composer of counterpoint). *Counterpoint* is the simultaneous presentation of two or more principal melody lines.
- **F.** Geminiani's Concerto Grosso in E Minor, op. 3, no. 3, published in London in 1732, is an example of the composer's contrapuntal craft.
    1. In this work, the concertino consists of four instruments: two violins, a viola, and a 'cello.
    2. The second movement is a fugue, initiated by the concertino and only eventually joined by the ripieno. Restatements of the fugue subject are usually played by the concertino, and the *episodes* (the passages of music between restatements of the fugue subject) are played by the ripieno. **Musical selection:**

Geminiani, Concerto Grosso in E Minor, op. 3, no. 3, movement 2.

III. Francesco Manfredini (1684–1762), from Pistoia, Italy, studied violin in Bologna with Torelli. His Concerto Grosso in C Major, op. 3, no. 12, published in Bologna in 1718, was, like Corelli's *Christmas* Concerto, written to be played at midnight mass on Christmas Eve.

   A. The concerto's first movement is in ritornello form. Labeled *Pastorale*, the movement evokes the shepherds at the birth of Christ through the use of a gentle *Siciliano*, a slowish peasant dance in triple meter of Sicilian origin.

   B. The opening ritornello theme is played by the tutti, followed by an extended episode for the concertino, which consists of two violins. **Musical selection:** Manfredini, Concerto Grosso in C Major, op. 3, no. 12, movement 1.

IV. Pietro Antonio Locatelli (1695–1764) was born in Bergamo in northern Italy. He synthesized almost every compositional style of the Baroque period, and his later work exhibits features of the Classical-era style, which had come into its own by the time of Locatelli's death in 1764.

   A. Locatelli studied with Corelli and, as a result, received a conservative Roman compositional education. This changed, however, when he traveled around Italy and became influenced by the new Venetian style of concerti, most notably those of Vivaldi. After moving to Amsterdam in 1729, he became one of the most important composers in Europe.

   B. Of Locatelli's published concerti, his op. 1 concerti are the most reflective of his conservative Roman training. Yet their rhythmic energy, melodic angularity, and lightness of spirit set them apart from any of the Baroque concerti we have thus far examined. **Musical selection:** Locatelli, Concerto Grosso in Bb Major, op. 1, no. 3, movement 5 (c. 1721).

   C. Locatelli's concerti are wonderfully quirky and wildly expressive, a characteristic that did not endear them to some of his contemporaries.

V. Georg Muffat (1653–1704) was the first non-Italian composer of significance. Trained as an organist, he studied with Jean-Baptiste Lully in Paris and completed his education in Vienna.

- A. Sometime around 1681–1682, Muffat left his position in Salzburg to study and work in Rome for about a year. There, he became inspired by Corelli's trio sonatas and concerti grossi and wrote some trio sonatas, scored, like Corelli's, for two violins, 'cello, and continuo. When Muffat returned to Salzburg, he published instructions on how to convert them into concerti grossi, including having the entire orchestra (both ripieno and concertino) play the sections marked "T" for tutti, and having the concertino play those sections marked with an "S" for solo.
- B. The fifth and final movement of the Concerto Grosso no. 5 in D Major (c. 1682) is a wonderful hybrid of the French and Italian styles, the two most important influences on Muffat's compositional style. The movement is a *minuet* (a stately French dance in triple meter), performed in the Italian concertato style by alternating concertino (soloists) and tutti (full ensemble). **Musical selection:** Muffat, Concerto Grosso no. 5 in D Major, movement 5.

VI. Georg Philipp Telemann (1681–1767) was one of the three greatest German-born composers of the High Baroque, the others being George Frederick Handel and Johann Sebastian Bach. Typical of High Baroque German music, theirs represents a synthesis of Italian and French musical genres and styles, marked by a singularly German intensity of expression and an emphasis on technique.
- A. Telemann's music is particularly reflective of this eclecticism. He was the music director for the city of Hamburg (the most prestigious musical position in the German-speaking world during the Baroque). He was the most prolific composer of his day and was considered in his lifetime to be the most important composer in German-speaking Europe.
- B. Telemann composed around 500 concerti, of which only just over 100 have survived. Most are relatively early works, composed before his move to Hamburg in 1721. We will sample four of them to get a sense of the range and variety of his concerti and to understand the degree to which his compositional style was a synthesis of Italian, French, German, and even Polish musical elements.
- C. Telemann's Concerto in D Major for Three *Corni di Caccia* (hunting horns) and Violin is a fascinating hybrid of concerto

grosso and solo concerto. The three horns are treated as a concertino, and the violin is treated as a soloist in its own right. The conclusion of the third and final movement is a brilliant example of Telemann's ability to blend and combine contrasting instrumental colors. **Musical selection:** Telemann, Concerto in D Major for Three Corni di Caccia and Violin, movement 3, conclusion. As a Baroque orchestrator, only Johann Sebastian Bach was Telemann's equal.

D. Between 1705 and 1708, Telemann was music director at the court of Sorau in Silesia (now the Polish city of Zary). He became fascinated by Polish folk music, whose influence is to be found in some of his concerti, including the *Concerto Polonais*, or *Polish Concerto in Bb Major* (c. 1715). This is a ripieno concerto: The entire first violin section plays the role of soloist. The first movement is a *polonaise*—a stately dance of Polish origin. **Musical selection:** Telemann, Concerto in Bb Major for Strings, movement 1, opening.

E. One of Telemann's great masterworks is his Concerto in E Major for Flute, Oboe d'amore, and Viola d'amore (c.1715). An *oboe d'amore* is an alto oboe, pitched a minor third below a standard oboe. A *viola d'amore* is a viola-sized instrument of the viol family.

  1. This concerto is a triple concerto (not a concerto grosso). The flute, oboe, and viola all behave as solo instruments; they are not integrated into a coherent concertino.

  2. The first movement begins with an incredibly nuanced and delicate passage with throbbing strings accompanying the flute, oboe d'amore, and viola d'amore as they each enter separately. **Musical selection:** Telemann, Concerto in E Major for Flute, Oboe d'amore, and Viola d'amore, movement 1, opening.

  3. The second-movement ritornello form has the lilt and snap of a folk dance. The third movement is a Siciliano featuring the viola d'amore. The fourth and final movement is dance-like and betrays the influence of Telemann's beloved Polish folk music. This concerto is one of the great masterworks of the High Baroque.

F. The third and final movement of Telemann's Oboe Concerto in F Minor is, like all of Telemann's best work, direct in expression and engaging in character, a marvelous synthesis of Italian form, French instrumental practice, and German precision. **Musical selection:** Telemann, Oboe Concerto in F Minor (arranged for trumpet), movement 3.

    G. Telemann and Johann Sebastian Bach had great respect for each other. Telemann did what he could to promote Bach's career, but his efforts were hampered by Bach's difficult personality and the fact that Bach's music was considered by his contemporaries to be too complicated. At his death in 1767, Telemann was succeeded in Hamburg by Bach's son, Carl Philipp Emanuel, or C. P. E. Bach.

VII. George Frederick Handel (1685–1759) was born in Halle in central Germany. He finished his musical education in the major opera centers of Italy. His Italian experience had a decisive influence on his compositional development. In 1712, he moved permanently to England, where he was lionized by the English, who eventually claimed him as *their* greatest composer.

    A. When in Italy, Handel was greatly influenced by Corelli's concerti. The majority of Handel's instrumental compositions were byproducts of his theater music, many of the concerto movements being adapted from vocal or instrumental numbers originally created for theatrical works.

    B. When the popularity of his Italian-style operas began to wane during the mid- and late 1730s, Handel began to write *oratorios* (operas based on religious subjects, intended for performance in the concert hall, and sung in English) and concerti.

    C. Handel's 12 concerti grossi of op. 6 betray the influence of Corelli and the Roman-style concerto grosso: They number between five and seven movements in length and are expressively restrained and lyric. Yet they are a wonderful synthesis of old and new: They combine the French overture; French, English, and Italian dances; fugue and theme and variations techniques; and operatic elements, such as aria, duet, and accompanied recitative.

    D. Handel's Concerto Grosso in Bb Major, op. 6, no. 7 is an example of the multinational nature of these concerti: The fifth and final movement is a *hornpipe*, a jig-like dance popular in Britain; the concerto grosso itself is in the Corelli-inspired Roman style, while its composer was German-born, Italian-trained, and lived in

London! **Musical selection:** Handel, Concerto Grosso in Bb Major, op. 6, no. 7, movement 5.

E. Handel's 12 "Grand" Concerti, op. 6, are among the great masterworks of Baroque instrumental music.

Lecture Four
Bach's *Brandenburg* Concerti

Scope: Thanks to the Amsterdam music publisher Etienne Roger, Italian concerti were known throughout Europe by the early 18th century, providing inspirational models for non-Italian composers. One such composer was Johann Sebastian Bach, who discovered Roger's editions of concerti by Vivaldi, Corelli, Marcello, and others in the library of his employer, the duke of Weimar. Bach learned from his Italian models and surpassed them in the breadth of his vision, the complexity of his thematic material, and his mastery of counterpoint. Bach's transcendental compositions marry craft, imagination, spiritual depth, and expressive profundity with lyricism, grace, and delicacy. These qualities, along with his extraordinary art in fusing national styles, can be found in the six concerti that are known as the *Brandenburg* concerti. Bach's concerti are supreme masterworks, unmatched by any concerti before those of Mozart.

Outline

I. A great many early concerti were published in Amsterdam by the firm of Etienne Roger, a French Protestant music printer who had fled Normandy in 1685. At that time, Louis XIV revoked the Edict of Nantes, which had guaranteed French Protestants protection from religious persecution. As a result, thousands of highly skilled Protestants, including Etienne Roger, left France for safer locales.

  A. Engraving and printing at that time was an expensive and highly specialized craft. Printers could not afford to have unsold music lying on their shelves. In his efforts to find marketable music, Etienne Roger took a major risk: By printing and publicizing them, Italian concerti could become very popular. Thanks to Roger, all Europe became acquainted with the "new" Italian concerti, including non-Italian composers, who were inspired to compose their own.

  B. In 1713, when he was serving as the court organist for the duke of Weimar, Johann Sebastian Bach discovered Roger's editions of concerti by Vivaldi, Corelli, Marcello, and others in the court library. Inspired by their freshness, lyricism, wit, and elegance, he arranged many of them for harpsichord. The impact of the Italian concerto on Bach's own compositional development was decisive.

II. The music of Johann Sebastian Bach (1685–1750) fulfilled Francesco Geminiani's prescription: "…to please the ear …express sentiments, strike the imagination, affect the mind, and command the passions."

   A. Bach was one of the most prodigiously gifted composers in the history of Western music. His art is a seamless marriage of transcendental craft and imagination, spiritual depth and expressive profundity, exquisite lyricism, grace, and delicacy. Furthermore, it is the preeminent example of the synthesis of national styles that marks the best of German Baroque music.

   B. Bach's six concerti for "diverse instruments"—the *Brandenburg* concerti—consist of four concerti grossi (nos. 1, 2, 4, and 5) and two ripieno concerti (nos. 3 and 6). The *Brandenburg* concerti were written at various times between 1717 (or earlier) and 1721 at the court of Anhalt-Cöthen, where Bach was employed.
      1. The court orchestra, numbering between 15 and 18 musicians, was one of the best in Europe; Bach himself played either viola or harpsichord, depending on the piece.
      2. Bach's employer, Prince Leopold I, selected the very finest musicians, and the cost went a long way toward bankrupting him.
      3. Bach composed many of his greatest concerti for this orchestra, before the prince was forced, for financial reasons, to disband it.

   C. Aware that his employer was in financial trouble, Bach began to look for a new position. He selected six of his concerti and sent them to the margrave of Brandenburg, Christian Ludwig, hoping that the margrave would be so impressed by them that he would offer Bach a position. Unfortunately, Bach did not even get a reply from the margrave. (For details of this episode in Bach's career, see Professor Greenberg's Teaching Company course entitled *Bach and the High Baroque*, Lectures Thirteen through Sixteen.)

III. Bach's *Brandenburg* Concerto no. 1 in F Major has four movements. (The others in the *Brandenburg* concerti have three movements.)

A. *Brandenburg* no. 1 is composed for the largest ensemble of any of this group of concerti. It is divided into three contrasting choirs: the first for two hunting horns; the second for three oboes and a bassoon; and the third for strings in six parts: a solo violino piccolo (small violin tuned, here, a minor third above the standard violin tuning), first and second violins, viola, 'cello, and bass.

B. The royal and celebratory first movement begins with a ritornello theme that is played by the tutti. **Musical selection:** Bach, *Brandenburg* Concerto no. 1 in F Major, BWV 1046 (c. 1719), movement 1, ritornello theme.

C. During the solo sections, the three choirs (horns, oboes, and strings) alternate and compete with each other and overlap, lead, and accompany each other in numerous ways. **Musical selection:** Bach, *Brandenburg* Concerto no. 1 in F Major, BWV 1046, movement 1, episode.

D. The lyric, completely Italian-styled second movement (*adagio*) features a solo oboe and the violino piccolo. **Musical selection:** Bach, *Brandenburg* Concerto no. 1 in F Major, BWV 1046, movement 2, opening.

E. The brilliant ritornello-form third movement could have ended the concerto nicely. **Musical selection:** Bach, *Brandenburg* Concerto no. 1 in F Major, BWV 1046, movement 3, ritornello theme.

F. Instead of ending the concerto here, Bach adds a minuet—a graceful, triple-meter dance of French origin—with two contrasting episodes, called *trios*. **Musical selection:** Bach, *Brandenburg* Concerto no. 1 in F Major, BWV 1046, movement 4, minuet.
   1. The first trio is scored for two oboes and a bassoon. **Musical selection:** Bach, *Brandenburg* Concerto no. 1 in F Major, BWV 1046, movement 4, trio 1.
   2. The second trio, marked *polacca* (Polish dance), is scored for two violins, viola, and continuo. **Musical selection:** Bach, *Brandenburg* Concerto no. 1 in F Major, BWV 1046, movement 4, trio 2.
   3. The minuet returns, and the movement and the concerto come to an end.

G. By adding the last movement, Bach made this first *Brandenburg* concerto an extremely unorthodox work: It evokes a French dance suite, which often ended with a minuet; it reflects the concerti of French-trained composers, such as Georg Muffat; and it acknowledges the Roman-style concerti grossi of Corelli, which usually had four to six movements and typically concluded with a dance movement. Bach also tips his hat to Telemann, whose own concerti often featured polaccas.

IV. The second *Brandenburg* concerto (c.1719) opens with a ritornello theme played by the tutti and punctuated by a series of solos by the instruments of the concertino—violin, treble recorder, oboe, and trumpet. (See Professor Greenberg's Teaching Company course *Bach and the High Baroque* for a detailed discussion of this work.) **Musical selection:** Bach, *Brandenburg* Concerto no. 2 in F Major, BWV 1047, movement 1.

   A. Its celebratory nature has much to do with its treble-dominated concertino. This particular set of instruments (violin, treble recorder, oboe, and trumpet) had never been used in a concerto grosso before and rarely, if ever, had a composer demanded so much from the valveless trumpet of that time.

   B. Bach's trumpet player for this piece, Johann Ludwig Schreiber, had a transcendently difficult part that required playing at the very top of the instrument's range (the so-called *clarino* register) almost all the time. With its brilliant sound and its virtuosic part, the trumpet is the lead player in the concertino, while the concertino itself dominates the music. **Musical selection:** Bach, *Brandenburg* Concerto no. 2 in F Major, BWV 1047, movement 3, fugue, opening.

   C. The trumpet takes a well-earned break during the second movement, a sublime *adagio*. **Musical selection:** Bach, *Brandenburg* Concerto no. 2 in F Major, BWV 1047, movement 2, opening.

V. *Brandenburg* Concerto no. 3 in G Major (c. 1718) is a ripieno concerto: It is scored for string orchestra and continuo only; there is no "featured" soloist or soloists. By definition, in a ripieno concerto, the first violins carry the bulk of the thematic weight.

   A. *Brandenburg* Concerto no. 3, however, is not a typical ripieno concerto. It is a true concerto for orchestra, as Bach divides the strings into three distinct and contrasting choirs: the violins, violas, and 'cellos, representing high, medium, and low voices. The material for each choir demands tremendous virtuosity from all the players—in essence, every player becomes a soloist.

   B. The first-movement ritornello theme, played by the tutti, is followed by solo sections that pit the various string choirs against each other. **Musical selection:** Bach, *Brandenburg* Concerto no. 3 in G Major, BWV 1048, movement 1. Bach brings out the sonorities of the strings with consummate artistry.

   C. There is no slow second movement, only two chords forming a Phrygian cadence. These chords most probably provided the support for a brief, improvised solo by one or more of the players.

   D. The high-speed third movement is a perpetual motion in the style of a *gigue*—a fast dance in compound duple meter. The virtuosity required of the tutti is breathtaking. **Musical selection:** Bach, *Brandenburg* Concerto no. 3 in G Major, BWV 1048, movement 3.

VI. *Brandenburg* Concerto no. 4 in G Major (c. 1719) is a concerto grosso with a high-pitched concertino, consisting of two treble recorders and a violin.

   A. The first movement is a triple-meter dance, as opposed to duple meter, which is much more usual for the first movement. It is pastoral in mood. **Musical selection:** Bach, *Brandenburg* Concerto no. 4 in G Major, BWV 1049, movement 1, opening.

   B. The solo violin is prominent in the first and third movements. In the first movement, the violin has three lengthy solos, the second of which is especially virtuosic. **Musical selection:** Bach, *Brandenburg* Concerto no. 4 in G Major, BWV 1049, movement 1, violin solo.

   C. In the second movement (*andante*), the concertino is absorbed into the larger ensemble. **Musical selection:** Bach, *Brandenburg* Concerto no. 4 in G Major, BWV 1049, movement 2, opening.

   D. As in the second *Brandenburg* concerto, the third movement of the fourth *Brandenburg* concerto is a lively fugue, but unlike the earlier work, this fugue is introduced by the ripieno. **Musical selection:** Bach, *Brandenburg* Concerto no. 4 in G Major, BWV 1049, movement 3, fugue, exposition, and solo violin–dominated concertino episode. The virtuosic violin passages in this movement give the impression that this concerto is a concerto grosso with the heart of a solo concerto.

VII. The fifth *Brandenburg* concerto also gives the impression of being part concerto grosso and part solo concerto, because of its dominant harpsichord part. The harpsichord is particularly dominant in the first movement, where it has an incredibly difficult, three-minute long cadenza. The story goes that Bach had purchased a new harpsichord for the court at Anhalt-Cöthen and used this first movement to "break it in." (For an in-depth discussion of this movement, see Professor Greenberg's Teaching Company course entitled *How to Listen to and Understand Great Music*.)

   A. We hear the extraordinary harpsichord cadenza and the subsequent statement of the ritornello theme that concludes the movement. **Musical selection:** Bach, *Brandenburg* Concerto no. 5 in D Major, BWV 1050 (c. 1721), movement 1, harpsichord cadenza and conclusion.

   B. The *Brandenburg* no. 5 is the first concerto ever composed with a solo keyboard part. In this work, Bach cut the harpsichord free from its role as an accompanying instrument. In doing so, Bach de facto invented the solo keyboard concerto, a genre with which he continued to experiment for the rest of his career.

VIII. The sixth and last of the *Brandenburg* concerti was likely the first to be composed. Current research indicates that it was first drafted in 1713, while Bach was working in Weimar. At that time, he was discovering the concerti of such composers as Vivaldi and Corelli.

   A. This concerto relies entirely on medium and low instrumental timbres. It is scored for two violas, two viole da gamba (an archaic instrument), 'cello, and harpsichord. This scoring gives the work a heavy, even somber quality.

   B. That the viole da gamba parts are simple is most likely attributable to the fact that Prince Leopold was a viole da gamba enthusiast, and Bach wisely composed playable parts for his employer.

   C. The ritornello-form first movement features a canon between the two violas, with a throbbing accompaniment provided by the rest of the ensemble. **Musical selection:** Bach, *Brandenburg* Concerto no. 6 in Bb Major, BWV 1051, movement 1, ritornello theme.

D. The "heaviness" of the orchestral register is especially noticeable in the second movement (*adagio*) scored for the two violas, 'cello, and continuo only. **Musical selection:** Bach, *Brandenburg* Concerto no. 6 in Bb Major, movement 2, opening.

E. The two violas are prominent in the gigue-like third movement, where they constitute a concertino, as in a concerto grosso. The ritornello theme is played by the two violas in unison and accompanied by the ripieno. Then, rapid solo lines in the violas alternate with fragments of the ritornello theme. **Musical selection:** Bach, *Brandenburg* Concerto no. 6 in Bb Major, BWV 1051, movement 3, ritornello theme.

IX. Bach took the straightforward alternation of solo and ripieno of the Italian concerto and transformed it into something far more complex and less predictable. There is no aspect of Bach's concerto composition—melody, harmony, form, dramatic impact, or instrumental virtuosity—that is not superior to that of his Italian models. Bach's concerti are first-rank masterworks and the greatest concerti composed before Mozart's.

Lecture Five
Mozart, Part 1

Scope: The mid-18th century saw the Enlightenment era come to full bloom and, with it, the aesthetic doctrine that the best music was music that appealed to the greatest number, a music that was well crafted and in good taste. In compositional terms, this meant melodic beauty and clarity, clear phrase structures and carefully balanced musical forms, and expressive restraint. With its emphasis on the importance of melody, this so-called Classical-era style demanded musical forms that could accommodate multiple themes, forms that stressed thematic contrast, departure, and return. Among the most significant innovations of Classical-era instrumental music were sonata form and double-exposition form, the version of sonata form used in concerto composition. The concerto, centered on the soloist, became a metaphor for the Enlightenment's emphasis on the value of the individual. The solo concerto became the predominant type of concerto during the Classical era. Mozart, the brightest star in the Classical firmament, was also, arguably, the greatest composer of concerti who ever lived.

Outline

I. Johann Wolfgang Christian Gottlieb Mozart (1756–1791) composed more masterworks in a greater range of genres than virtually any composer before or after him. Together with Bach, Mozart possessed the most prodigious compositional technique and the most exquisite imagination in the history of Western music.

    A. Mozart's art, characterized by pure, natural lyricism; dramatic timing; depth of expression; and technical mastery of phrase structure and harmony, allows him to convey, in the words of musicologist Maynard Solomon "a sense of discovery."

    B. Mozart's greatest ambition was to compose operas. In his day, opera was the single most prestigious, profitable, and exciting medium in existence. Mozart was a great opera composer; he had an instinct for drama: He thought in terms of thematic contrasts, developments, and reconciliation. Whether he was writing vocal or instrumental music, he constantly thought about scenario, the interplay of and relationship between contrasting musical elements. He was a genius of the theater.

- **C.** The same skills that made Mozart a genius of an opera composer made him the greatest composer of concerti. He composed more than 40 concerti, including more than 20 for keyboard, 5 for violin, and 4 for horn, in addition to concerti for flute, flute and harp, oboe, bassoon, clarinet, and many more.
- **D.** The goals of this lecture and the next are to:
    1. Discuss the Enlightenment and its impact on musical style.
    2. Observe the vast difference between the cyclic, ritornello-based musical forms of the Baroque era and the linear, narrative-based musical forms of the Classical-era.
    3. Observe the preeminence of the solo concerto over other types of concerti during the Classical-era.
    4. Explore and sample Mozart's extraordinary output of concerti, in particular, his concerti for piano.

II. Mozart's era was that of the Enlightenment of the mid-18th century, when the growing middle classes in Europe began to exert a significant influence on social developments and the individual became an essential unit in society—aristocrats still ruled Europe but now, to some extent, became more concerned for the well-being of their subjects.

- **A.** The Enlightenment promoted the belief that something is good if it does the greatest good for the greatest number. In the world of music, this doctrine of accessibility defined the best music as music that appealed to the greatest number, providing it was well written and in good taste. This music of the Enlightenment—known as the Classical era of music—came to celebrate:
    1. Melodic beauty and clarity.
    2. Balance and purity of form (clear phrase structures and carefully balanced musical forms).
    3. Expressive restraint and good taste (meaning purity of conception and expression).
- **B.** Typical for his time, Mozart composed no concerti grossi. The sort of "group think" represented by the concertino had little spiritual or intellectual context in the age of the Enlightenment. Nor did he

write ripieno concerti—by the mid-18th century, this genre evolved into the symphony. But he *was* a man of his time in writing solo concerti. The Enlightenment's emphasis on the individual found its musical metaphor in the solo concerto, centered, as it is, on the individual musical voice.

III. As a performer, Mozart was best known in his day for his piano playing, but he was also an accomplished violinist. His virtuosic violin concerti, which he most likely composed for himself, are molded to the temperament and idiosyncrasies of both the instrument and the player. Mozart completed five violin concerti, the first probably written in 1773 and the rest between June 14 and December 20, 1775. To appreciate both Classical-era and Romantic concerti, we need to understand some basic differences between Baroque and Classical-era musical forms.

  A. Baroque instrumental music is characteristically monothematic, cyclical, and continuous.
  1. Movements in Baroque music are, with rare exceptions, monothematic: built from and organized around a single theme. Thematic contrasts occur between movements, rather than between themes within one movement.
  2. Baroque instrumental procedures, such as fugue and ritornello form, feature a single theme that returns, in its entirety or as fragments, in cycles. Episodic material is constructed from fragments of the fugue or ritornello theme.
  3. Rhythmic continuity—maintaining momentum—is key in any Baroque movement.

  B. These three characteristics of Baroque music do not apply to Classical-era music. With Classical-era music's emphasis on vocally conceived, memorable, and accessible melodies, a new set of musical forms emerged that were multi-thematic, narrative, and discontinuous.
  1. During the mid-18th century, new musical forms evolved, and older Baroque forms were adapted to the new Enlightenment-inspired, Classical-era view of melody. These forms employed multiple themes and stressed thematic contrast, departure, and return.

2. Dialogue between contrasting themes creates tension—dramatic conflict—that implies a storyline, a narrative, across the span of a movement.
3. Classical-era movements are full of pauses and moments of acceleration and deceleration as themes are introduced, transited to, juxtaposed, and developed. The rhythmic flexibility of Classical-era music imbues it with a rhetorical sensibility akin to storytelling, as opposed to the more motoric, dance-like rhythmic momentum of most Baroque instrumental music.

IV. The most important formal innovation of Classical-era music was the invention of sonata form, sometimes called *sonata-allegro form*.
   A. *Sonata form* is the structure of a movement in which two or more principal themes are introduced, developed, and recapitulated in their original order.
      1. The first large section of a sonata-form movement, in which the themes are introduced, is called the *exposition*.
      2. The second large section of a sonata-form movement, in which the themes are developed, is called, logically, the *development section*.
      3. The third large section of a sonata-form movement, in which the themes return in their original order, is called the *recapitulation*.
      4. A fourth section—a *coda*— is added to the end of the movement to create a sense of conclusion.
   B. In the exposition, the contrasting themes are introduced in different keys, and in performance, the exposition is usually repeated in its entirety to familiarize the listener with the themes and their keys.
   C. Almost every first movement of a Classical-era instrumental composition is in sonata form, as are many final movements and even some middle movements. Sonata form was also adapted to the needs of the Classical-era solo concerto. This version is known as *double-exposition form*.

V. Mozart brought double-exposition form to a level of perfection that ensured that it would remain a feature of concerto structure well into the 20th century. We turn to Mozart's Violin Concerto no. 4 in D Major, K. 218 (1775), as an example of double-exposition form.

A. Like the Venetian-inspired concerti of the High Baroque, the Classical-era concerto is a three-movement construct, following a tempo scheme of fast–slow–fast.

B. Mozart's Violin Concerto no. 4 in D Major, like virtually every Classical-era concerto, begins with a double-exposition-form first movement.

C. The double-exposition form features two separate expositions, neither of which is repeated. (Remember, in sonata form, there is one exposition that is repeated.)
   1. In the first exposition—the orchestral exposition—the orchestra plays the themes.
   2. In the second exposition—the solo exposition—the soloist plays the themes.

D. In the orchestral exposition of the first movement of Mozart's Violin Concerto no. 4 in D Major, the upbeat first theme begins with a fanfare played by the tutti. **Musical selection:** Mozart, Violin Concerto no. 4 in D Major, K. 218, movement 1, orchestral exposition, theme 1, bridge (brief transition), and pause.
   1. The pause that concludes that excerpt is exactly the sort of discontinuity that is characteristic of the rhetorical nature of Classical-era music. It anticipates a new and contrasting theme; it is a moment of rest before the narrative resumes.
   2. The sinuous second theme that immediately follows the pause is initially heard in the strings. It features a loud and rather unexpected rising idea at the end of each of its phrases. **Musical selection:** Mozart, Violin Concerto no. 4 in D Major, K. 218, movement 1, theme 2.
   3. There is a sly sort of humor here that is characteristic of all Mozart's violin concerti. It suggests that these concerti, which Mozart performed himself, get as close to Mozart's own voice and sense of humor as any of his works.
   4. The orchestral exposition concludes with a vigorous *cadence* (closing music), followed by a pause. **Musical selection:** Mozart, Violin Concerto no. 4 in D Major, K. 218, movement 1, cadence material.

E. The solo exposition features modified versions of the themes. The formerly martial-sounding first theme is now heard high in the violin's range, giving it a sweet, feminine character. **Musical selection:** Mozart, Violin Concerto no. 4 in D Major, K. 218, movement 1, solo exposition, theme 1.
   1. There follows the kind of innovation that Mozart brought to double-exposition form: The soloist does not proceed immediately to the second theme but introduces an entirely new theme. This will be the soloist's exclusive theme—literally, a "solo theme." **Musical selection:** Mozart, Violin Concerto no. 4 in D Major, K. 218, movement 1, solo exposition, solo theme/theme 3.
   2. Next, the soloist plays an extended version of theme 2 but with a difference. Unlike regular sonata form, double-exposition form presents both themes *in the same key* in the orchestral exposition. Only in the solo exposition will theme 2 be heard in its own contrasting key. **Musical selection:** Mozart, Violin Concerto no. 4 in D Major, K. 218, movement 1, solo exposition, theme 2 extended, and cadence material.
   3. This sort of harmonic manipulation is a key element of Mozart's musical language, and it is the reason that the repetition of music (in a different key from the original) sounds fresh and even new.

F. Next comes the development section, in which the themes are metamorphosed, juxtaposed, and blended over a constantly changing harmonic accompaniment. A concerto development usually provides the soloist with virtuosic material.

G. The recapitulation in a double-exposition-form movement behaves like the recapitulation in sonata form: The two principal themes return in their original order, both in the home key. Double-exposition form adds the reappearance of the third theme (solo theme), which can appear anywhere. In this concerto, the solo theme (played, of course, by the violin) initiates the recapitulation, after which themes 1 and 2 are heard.

H. The final feature of double-exposition form to be discussed is the *cadenza* (*cadence*, in English). A cadence is a harmonic formula that occurs near the end of a phrase, section, or movement, signaling a temporary or permanent conclusion. By Mozart's time, it had become standard concerto procedure to allow the soloist to perform an extended solo, named *cadenza* for the harmonic progression it interrupts.

I. Mozart did not compose cadenzas for his violin concerti; the soloist is supposed to provide one. Famous violinists have composed cadenzas for Mozart's violin concerti that are still used by performers. Many soloists, however, prefer to compose their own cadenzas to dazzle audiences with their virtuosity and exploit their particular skills.

J. At the conclusion of the recapitulation in the first movement of Mozart's Violin Concerto no. 4 in D Major, K. 218, the orchestra plays the cadence material; then, a series of harmonies constitutes the final cadence, which comes to rest on a cadential six-four chord. This is the standard Classical-era chord that precedes the cadenza and is a familiar sound in Classical concerti. The cadenza itself follows and ends with a trill, signaling that the soloist has finished the cadenza. After this, the two final chords of the final cadence conclude the movement. **Musical selection:** Mozart, Violin Concerto no. 4 in D Major, K. 218, movement 1, recapitulation, cadence material, cadenza, and conclusion.

VI. Another example of double-exposition form is to be found in Mozart's Flute Concerto no. 1 in G Major, K. 313 (1778).

    A. Mozart did not particularly like the flute. Nevertheless, he did not turn down a generous commission from a wealthy amateur flute player named Ferdinand de Jean, who commissioned four flute concerti and six quartets for flute and strings. Despite his claim to detest the flute, Mozart produced some of the most gorgeous and idiomatic music ever written for the instrument.

    B. We will listen to alternations of the orchestral and solo expositions to hear the different versions of the themes. **Musical selections:** Mozart, Flute Concerto in G Major, K. 313, movement 1, orchestral exposition, theme 1; movement 1, solo exposition, theme 1; movement 1, orchestral exposition, theme 2; movement 1, solo exposition, theme 2; movement 1, orchestral exposition, cadence material; movement 1, solo exposition, cadence material; movement 1, solo exposition, solo theme.

    C. Be aware of the huge and wonderful contrast between both expositions, a contrast inherent in double-exposition form. The orchestral exposition is declamatory and symphonic, while the solo exposition is much more intimate. The contrast between the soloist and the orchestra, between the individual and the collective, takes on a metaphorical meaning that is relative to our own lives and goes beyond anything we experience in the orchestral exposition. **Musical selection:** Mozart, Flute Concerto in G Major, K. 313, movement 1, orchestral and solo expositions.

D. Finally, we hear the end of the recapitulation—the cadence material and the cadential six-four chord on which the music pauses; then, the cadenza, ending with a trill, and the conclusion of the movement. **Musical selection:** Mozart, Flute Concerto in G Major, K. 313, movement 1, end of recapitulation, cadence material, cadenza, and conclusion.

Lecture Six
Mozart, Part 2

Scope: This lecture focuses on the essentially collaborative nature of Mozart's concerti and his skill in shaping the music to complement the idiosyncrasies of the solo instrument and its performer. We also note the element of theatricality in Mozart's mature concerti, which imbues the solo instrument with a personality of its very own. The concerti exemplifying these characteristics and discussed in this lecture are the Oboe Concerto in C Major, K. 271k; Horn Concerto in Eb Major, K. 495; Sinfonia Concertante in Eb Major for Violin, Viola and Orchestra, K. 364; Concerto in Eb Major for Two Pianos, K. 365; Piano Concerto no. 20 in D Minor, K. 466; Piano Concerto no. 21 in C Major, K. 467; and Clarinet Concerto in A Major, K. 622.

Outline

I. The goals for this lecture are: to observe the collaborative relationship between soloist and orchestra in Mozart's concerti, to examine the degree to which Mozart's concerti are perfectly cast to the idiosyncrasies of the solo instrument and the performers for whom the concerti were composed, and to discuss the 17 piano concerti that Mozart composed between 1781 and 1791, each one a masterwork of the first order.

   A. Like the Baroque Italian composers who invented the concerto in the late 17th century, Mozart believed in the human voice and its lyric, expressive capabilities. He had a genius for vocally conceived melody.

   B. In the operas of Mozart's day, the singers and their music were of preeminent importance; the opera orchestra was there to provide an unobtrusive accompaniment to the singers.

   C. In Mozart's concerti, the same collaborative approach is taken. The potential conflicts of the concertato style are almost completely foreign to Mozart's compositional style, as are the sorts of confrontations we will hear in Beethoven's concerti. The hallmarks of Mozart's mature style are balance, lyricism, elegance, and good taste.

II. The second goal of this lecture, to examine the degree to which Mozart's concerti are perfectly molded to the idiosyncrasies of the solo instruments and the soloist, is exemplified by Mozart's Oboe Concerto in C Major, K. 271k (1777).
   A. Mozart lavished a lot of great music on the woodwinds in a wide range of genres. His Oboe Concerto in C Major was composed in Salzburg in 1777 for the principal oboist of the Salzburg court orchestra, Giuseppe Ferlendis. Late in 1777, Mozart showed his oboe concerto to Friedrich Ramm, the oboist in the Mannheim orchestra and one of the greatest oboists of all time. Ramm was, to use Mozart's word, "crazy" about the concerto.
   B. The third and final movement is a rondo. Like ritornello form, rondo form is a refrain-type procedure, in which the principal theme (the rondo theme) alternates with various contrasting themes and/or episodes. The rondo theme is played alternately by the oboe and the orchestra. Mozart's orchestral accompaniment is incredibly deft. He uses the full range of the oboe and a variety of articulation, from individually tongued notes to sweeping groups of slurred notes. The recording used for this excerpt features a period oboe, built in Dresden in 1783. **Musical selection:** Mozart, Oboe Concerto in C Major, K. 271k/314, movement 3, rondo theme.
   C. Mozart arranged this concerto for flute in 1778 as one of the two flute concerti commissioned by Ferdinand de Jean. The flute version for de Jean survived, but the oboe version was lost until 1920!

III. Mozart's four horn concerti were all written for Joseph Leutgeb, principal horn player in Salzburg and a friend of Mozart. Leutgeb was a great virtuoso. He played the valveless horn (valves were not added until around 1820), which is a notoriously difficult instrument.
   A. The third and final movement of Mozart's Concerto for Horn in Eb, K. 495 (1786), is a rondo, with a theme inspired by the hunting horn. The following recorded excerpt features a natural (valveless) horn. **Musical selection:** Mozart, Horn Concerto in Eb Major, K. 495, movement 3, rondo theme. (This selection is played twice.)
   B. Mozart's music is so perfectly tailored to the vagaries and limitations of the natural horn that we are never aware of them. He maximizes the capabilities of the instrument without asking it to do

the impossible. **Musical selection:** Mozart, Horn Concerto in Eb Major, K. 495, movement 3 (in its entirety).

IV. Mozart composed his Concerto in C Major for Flute and Harp, K. 299, in 1778 while in Paris. It was commissioned by Adrien-Louis Bonnière de Soustre, count of Guines, who was a flute player. His daughter played the harp. The count never paid Mozart for the work, which is a masterpiece of lyric beauty and technical complexity.

  A. This concerto's slow second movement is a glowing aria for flute and harp. Mozart omits oboes and horns in this movement so that they cannot compete with the exquisitely delicate sound created by the two soloists. **Musical selection:** Mozart, Concerto in C Major for Flute and Harp, K. 299, movement 2, opening. Incredibly, Mozart wrote this concerto when he was only 22 years old!

  B. The reason that this concerto, with its multiple soloists, is not a concerto grosso is that the flute and harp are not treated as a unit (that is, as a concertino). Nor do they vie with the orchestra for dominance. Rather, each instrument is a true and independent soloist. We could properly call this concerto a "double" concerto for flute and harp.

V. Mozart's Sinfonia Concertante in Eb Major for Violin, Viola and Orchestra, K. 364, is not a concerto grosso either. A *sinfonia concertante* is a concertato-style symphony—a symphonic work featuring two or more soloists. The genre originated in Paris, and hundreds of such works were composed in the 1770s and 1780s.

  A. Mozart's Sinfonia Concertante in Eb Major was composed in Salzburg during the summer of 1779.

  B. The third and final movement of this work is in double-exposition form. The orchestra introduces the principal themes, which are then echoed and elaborated by the violin and viola. **Musical selection:** Mozart, Sinfonia Concertante in Eb Major, K. 364, movement 3, opening.

VI. In 1778–1779, Mozart focused on exploring the musical and dramatic possibilities inherent in concerti for more than one solo instrument. In addition to the Concerto for Flute and Harp, K. 299, and the Sinfonia Concertante, K. 364, he wrote the Concerto in Eb Major for Two Pianos.

- **A.** As children, Mozart and his sister frequently performed together keyboard music for four hands—on two harpsichords or as a duet on one harpsichord. Mozart wrote his Concerto for Two Pianos (or Harpsichords) in Eb Major for himself and his sister.
- **B.** The third and final movement is a rondo. The rondo theme is a two-step dance that musicologist Cuthbert Girdlestone identified as a French *ariette*. The movement begins with the orchestra playing the rondo theme. Then, the pianos enter as a single instrument for the first contrasting episode. They next initiate the first restatement of the rondo theme, which in turn, yields to a dark, dramatic, minor-mode second contrasting episode. **Musical selection:** Mozart, Concerto in Eb Major for Two Pianos, K. 365, movement 3, opening through beginning of second contrasting episode.

VII. Although Mozart's piano concerti are numbered 1–27, nos. 1–4 are actually arrangements of works by other composers. They were arranged, primarily, by Mozart's father, Leopold, for the young Mozart's early concert tours. Mozart's concerti for two pianos and for three pianos are also included in the count. Without the arrangements and the concerti for multiple pianos, we are left with 21 piano concerti. The final 17—nos. 11–27— were composed between 1781 and 1791, when Mozart lived in Vienna. Most of them were written for concerts at which Mozart was the featured soloist and the producer.

- **A.** Mozart elevated the keyboard concerto to a preeminent position above that of even the violin—a position it continues to hold to this day.
- **B.** Coincidental with Mozart's maturity as a composer was the piano's first period of maturity. It became Mozart's personal instrumental vehicle. He was fascinated by the piano's dramatic and expressive potential. As a body of work, Mozart's piano concerti are not just his greatest concerti, but quantitatively and qualitatively, they are the greatest set of concerti ever composed.
- **C.** Mozart's Piano Concerti no. 20 in D Minor and no. 21 in C Major were written between mid-January and early March of 1785, when Mozart was at the height of his popularity in Vienna. Although conceived together, they are poles apart in their moods. The D-minor work is dark and tragic, and the C-major work is brilliant and lyric.

D. These concerti were composed for Mozart's own use during the Lenten season of 1785. During Lent, opera performances were forbidden in Catholic cities, such as Vienna. As a result, Lent became the prime season for concerts of instrumental music, which was not forbidden.

E. The Piano Concerto in D Minor was the first of only two concerti that Mozart set in a minor key. The first theme of its double-exposition-form first movement does not act like a Classical-era theme. More rhythm than melody, the theme consists of two elements: a series of throbbing syncopations in the upper strings and an ominous series of motives in the low strings. Slowly, the strings rise and break free. **Musical selection:** Mozart, Piano Concerto no. 20 in D Minor, K. 466, movement 1, orchestral exposition, theme 1.

   1. The piano entry at the beginning of the second exposition is spectacular: It plays, for 11 measures, a quiet and forlorn tune, *unaccompanied*, conveying a profound sense of isolation. When the orchestra enters with theme 1, the piano becomes an active participant in this dark, dramatic music. In this recording, we hear a replica of Mozart's own piano built by Anton Walter during the early 1780s. **Musical selection:** Mozart, Piano Concerto no. 20 in D Minor, K. 466, movement 1, solo exposition, theme 1.

   2. The piano in this first movement is nothing less than a metaphor for the voice of humanity: a voice in the wilderness that becomes, by extension, each of our voices. It is all unreservedly operatic. It is no surprise to know that Beethoven was famous for his performances of this concerto and that the cadenzas he composed for it—Mozart did not write any of his own—continue to be played to this day.

F. The Piano Concerto no. 21 is a very different piece—a big, festive work that includes trumpets and drums and begins with a march-like theme that quickly takes on the character of a triumphal procession. **Musical selection:** Mozart, Piano Concerto no. 21 in C Major, K. 467, movement 1, orchestral exposition, theme 1.

   1. The spirit of grandeur that pervades the orchestral exposition cannot be maintained during the solo exposition; the pianos of Mozart's time were simply too small. Instead, Mozart creates for the solo piano the contrasting persona of a rakish bon vivant. First, we hear the last fanfarish version of theme 1 in the orchestral exposition. **Musical selection:** Mozart, Piano Concerto no. 21 in C Major, K. 467, movement 1, orchestral exposition, conclusion.

  2. The piano is now "escorted" on stage by three "lovely ladies": a sultry redhead, portrayed by a solo oboe; a husky-voiced brunette, portrayed by a solo bassoon; and a ravishing blond, portrayed by a solo flute. **Musical selection:** Mozart, Piano Concerto no. 21 in C Major, K. 467, movement 1, solo exposition, introduction.
  3. The soloist prepares in a highly theatrical fashion for the performance ahead. **Musical selection:** Mozart, Piano Concerto no. 21 in C Major, K. 467, movement 1, solo exposition, introduction.
  4. Theme 1 reappears, this time in a delicate, whimsical, almost balletic version, beginning with a trill heard over the strings. Mozart's orchestral accompaniment is always complementary; the piano never has to raise its voice to be heard. **Musical selection:** Mozart, Piano Concerto no. 21 in C Major, K. 467, movement 1, solo exposition, theme 1.
  5. Mozart's concerti K. 466 and K. 467, like all of Mozart's mature concerti, have a theatricality in which the solo instrument becomes a personality unto itself. No one before Mozart had ever written concerti like that.

VIII. Mozart's last completed work was finished in mid-November 1791, just a few weeks before his death on December 5, 1791. This clarinet concerto, along with virtually all Mozart's music for solo clarinet, was inspired by and written for the virtuoso clarinetist Anton Stadler.

  A. Mozart composed both his Clarinet Concerto in A Major and his Clarinet Quintet in A Major for a basset clarinet (a slightly extended clarinet), an instrument that Stadler designed and had built for his own performances. **Musical selection:** Mozart, Clarinet Concerto in A Major, K. 622, movement 3, opening.

  B. It took 4.6 billion years to create the genetic and environmental conditions necessary for Mozart to exist. It can be argued that his is the music of our universe, through which we can understand ourselves; it is eternal.

Lecture Seven
Classical Masters

Scope: The history of the concerto, as with history in general, is not a straightforward process, with one "event" immediately affecting the next in a simple linear progression. In the case of Mozart's concerti, it took several years for his work to have an impact on more than just a small circle of admirers and pupils. He had no influence on most of his contemporaries, a huge number of whom wrote a huge number of concerti, most of which have been lost. But Mozart's concerti and those of Beethoven were only possible because of the rich musical environments in which those two masters lived and worked. This lecture will focus on a few of those composers whose works contributed to the rich environment of pre-Classical and Classical-era concerti: Giuseppe Tartini, whose dazzling virtuosity as a violinist is seen in his concerti; Johann Joachim Quantz, a flute virtuoso whose style exhibits elements of both the pre-Classical and the Classical eras; Frederick II of Prussia, Quantz's gifted pupil; Johann Christian Bach, who was perhaps the single most important musical influence on Mozart; and Joseph Haydn, "father" of the symphony and string quartet, whose Trumpet Concerto in Eb Major is considered the greatest of his surviving concerti.

Outline

I. History is not as neat and linear as historians sometimes portray it. Events are often complex and contradictory.

    A. The history of the concerto is no different. Mozart's concerti, for example, had to wait until the 19th century, well after his death in 1791, to have their impact. The eminent musicologist H. C. Robbins Landon makes an important point when he writes that only "some of Mozart's piano concerti were played by admirers and pupils… [Mozart] had no influence on most of Europe's leading composers [of concerti]" (Layton, p. 57).

    B. Concerti were composed in huge numbers by an equally huge number of composers, although most of them have been lost. It is estimated that no more than five percent of the concerti composed during the mid- and late 18th century are available today; they were never published and have since been lost. Yet masterworks by Mozart and Beethoven were only possible because of the rich musical environments in which they worked.

II. Giuseppe Tartini (1692–1770) was one of the most important musicians of his time: composer, violinist, teacher, and music theorist of great influence and renown.

- **A.** Destined by his parents for a career in the priesthood, Tartini rebelled and provoked the ire of church authorities when he married. He found asylum at the monastery of the Friars Minor Conventual, where he studied composition. In 1715, he was pardoned and was reunited with his wife. From then on, his career as violinist, teacher, and composer took off.
- **B.** Tartini became such a famous violin virtuoso that his style of performance came to be known as the "Tartini style." It is reflected in his concerti.
- **C.** He wrote Venetian-style, three-movement concerti. Sometimes, he wrote two middle movements, allowing musicians the choice of which to perform, as in his Violin Concerto in A Major.
- **D.** Very few of Tartini's concerti were published in his lifetime, and he did not date his compositions. Based on the pre-Classical-era, aria-like nature of its themes, we can guess that the Violin Concerto in A Major was composed sometime in the 1750s.
- **E.** It is in his slow movements that Tartini best anticipates the Classical future and best demonstrates his essential maxim as a violinist: "To play well, one must sing well." The *largo andante* slow movement of the Violin Concerto in A Major is prefaced with this inscription: "Like streams, springs, rivers, flow bitter tears until my cruel grief is spent" (Layton, ed., *A Companion to the Concerto*). **Musical selection:** Tartini, Violin Concerto in A Major, D. 96, movement 4.

III. Johann Joachim Quantz (1697–1773) began his career as an oboist. In 1718, he was appointed oboist to the court of Augustus II, king of Poland and elector of Saxony. Six years later, he changed his instrument and became one of Europe's greatest flute players.

- **A.** In 1728, Frederick II, crown prince of Prussia, heard Quantz perform in Berlin and immediately arranged to take flute lessons with him. When Frederick became king of Prussia in 1740, he made Quantz court composer and conductor at Sanssouci, the royal residence in Potsdam, and Quantz continued to teach Frederick flute and composition.

B. Frederick was a music enthusiast and was estimated to have participated in more than 10,000 performances during his reign. Quantz composed more than 300 flute concerti for performance by himself and Frederick. They are among the most brilliant works every written for the instrument.

C. Stylistically, Quantz's music, like that of Tartini, treads a line between Baroque and Classical practice. The most obvious Baroque element is the presence of a harpsichord-led basso continuo. However, Quantz leans toward what would become known as the Classical style in his use of repeated melodic ideas within his themes, his relatively slow harmonic turnover, and his general avoidance of complex polyphonic textures.

D. This is exemplified in the third and final movement of his Flute Concerto in D Major (c. 1755), subtitled "For Potsdam." It is a ritornello-form movement with an infectious theme. The orchestra plays the ritornello theme, then the flute, followed by the first solo episode, which is brilliant and whimsical. After that, the orchestra returns with the ritornello theme. **Musical selection:** Quantz, Flute Concerto in D Major, movement 3.

E. In 1752, Quantz wrote a book on flute playing that also offers advice on how to judge a musician and a musical composition. Quantz specified that the third movement of a concerto should make a contrast with the first movement and contain a short, "fiery," and "playful" ritornello, while the solo part should be "pleasing, fleeting, and light." Quantz's D Major Concerto satisfies these criteria, as does the third and final movement of a concerto by his composition student, Frederick the Great of Prussia.

F. Frederick wrote four flute concerti, which he would have performed himself. We listen to the first half of the third and final movement of Frederick's Flute Concerto in C Major (c. 1755). **Musical selection:** Frederick II of Prussia, Flute Concerto no. 3 in C Major, movement 3.

IV. The Bach family of Thuringia in central Germany produced more than 80 professional *kapellmeisters*, culminating with Johann Sebastian Bach.

    A. Four of Bach's sons were particularly important composers, especially of pre-Classical concerti: Wilhelm Friedmann Bach, Carl Phillip Emanuel Bach, Johann Christoph Friedrich Bach, and Johann Christian Bach.

    B. Johann Christian Bach (J. C. Bach, 1735–1782), the 11th and last son of Johann Sebastian Bach, was the single most important musical influence on the young Wolfgang Mozart and the inventor of double-exposition form.

    C. The Piano Concerto in Eb Major, op. 7, no. 5, published in 1770, is still the most frequently performed of J. C. Bach's keyboard concerti.

        1. Theme 1 of the orchestral exposition of the first movement is a stately tune heard over a thrumming pedal (a repeated note in the bass). **Musical selection:** Johann Christian Bach, Piano Concerto in Eb Major, op. 7, no. 5, movement 1, orchestral exposition, theme 1.

        2. J. C. Bach combined the technical brilliance of his father with the direct and lyric musical ethos of the Enlightenment and, thereby, became one of the founders of the so-called Classical style. Mozart developed J. C. Bach's model, lengthening, intensifying, and rendering profound what had been more decorative than deep.

        3. A bridge passage connects theme 1 and theme 2 but does not change the key, as would happen in sonata form. (Remember, in double-exposition form, the new key [contrasting key] is saved for the soloist.) **Musical selection:** Johann Christian Bach, Piano Concerto in Eb Major, op. 7, no. 5, movement 1, orchestral exposition, bridge.

        4. Theme 2, still in the home key of Eb major, is a graceful, dancing tune; it merges seamlessly with the cadence material that brings the orchestral exposition to a conclusion. **Musical selection:** Johann Christian Bach, Piano Concerto in Eb Major, op. 7, no. 5, movement 1, orchestral exposition, theme 2 and cadence material.

        5. Unlike Mozart's typically theatrical solo entries, J. C. Bach's soloist enters simply and directly, playing a slightly

embellished version of the opening phrase of theme 1 before being joined by the orchestra. This recorded excerpt features a piano built in the 1780s. **Musical selection:** Johann Christian Bach, Piano Concerto in Eb Major, op. 7, no. 5, movement 1, solo exposition, theme 1.
  6. The bridge follows, and this time, it is a modulating bridge—it does not merely transit to the next theme but changes key in the process. **Musical selection:** Johann Christian Bach, Piano Concerto in Eb Major, op. 7, no. 5, movement 1, solo exposition, modulating bridge.
  7. Bach allows the solo piano to introduce a third theme (the solo theme), a procedure that will become a trademark feature of Mozart's piano concerti. Bach's theme is in the new key of Bb major. **Musical selection:** Johann Christian Bach, Piano Concerto in Eb Major, op. 7, no. 5, movement 1, solo exposition, theme 3.
  8. Theme 2 is now played by the soloist and the orchestra. **Musical selection:** Johann Christian Bach, Piano Concerto in Eb Major, op. 7, no. 5, movement 1, solo exposition, theme 2.
  9. The solo exposition then comes to a conclusion with cadence material. **Musical selection:** Johann Christian Bach, Piano Concerto in Eb Major, op. 7, no. 5, movement 1, solo exposition, cadence material.
  10. J. C. Bach's piano part in this concerto is straightforward and generally thematic; it lacks the elaborate passages that celebrate virtuosity for its own sake, which would soon be a hallmark of the piano concerto. Bach treats the solo piano more like a "featured member" of the orchestra than as a "coloratura soloist" standing out from the orchestra. Virtuosity is the exception rather than the rule in this work.

V. Joseph Haydn (1732–1809), the "father" of the symphony and the string quartet, wrote about 35 concerti, most of which have been lost. His reputation as a composer of concerti rests on three works: the Concerto in D Major for Harpsichord or Piano of 1784, the 'Cello Concerto in C Major of 1765, and the Trumpet Concerto in Eb Major of 1796.

  A. The trumpet concerto was Haydn's last purely instrumental composition and is generally considered the greatest of his surviving concerti.

B. It was inspired by Haydn's friend Anton Weidinger (1767–1852), a trumpet player with the Viennese court orchestra. Weidinger invented a keyed trumpet in 1793. It allowed him to play a full range of pitches much more easily than the unkeyed trumpets that had existed to that time. The keyed trumpet, however, never became popular and was replaced by the valved trumpet, which first appeared in 1813 and has since become standard.

1. The first movement of Haydn's Trumpet Concerto in Eb Major is in double-exposition form. Weidinger's audiences must have been amazed when he began to play. The keyless, valveless trumpet, like the clarino trumpets of the Baroque, could play only melodies with adjacent pitches in the upper register, where the natural harmonics lie closer together. In the lower and middle registers, a keyless, valveless trumpet can play only open, fanfare-type melodies, such as the reveille and taps. Weidinger's keyed trumpet could play in the middle register. **Musical selection:** Haydn, Trumpet Concerto in Eb Major, movement 1, solo exposition.

2. The second movement (*andante*) in Ab major is glowing and pastoral, and like the first movement, it exploits the trumpet's newly created middle register. **Musical selection:** Haydn, Trumpet Concerto in Eb Major, movement 2, opening.

3. The third movement is a fantastic rondo. Haydn's rondo theme is upbeat and instantly memorable. **Musical selection:** Haydn, Trumpet Concerto in Eb Major, movement 3, rondo theme.

4. The first contrasting episode, which begins in the darker harmonic key of C minor, is followed by a return of the rondo theme, featuring a wonderful dialogue between the trumpet and the solo flute. **Musical selection:** Haydn, Trumpet Concerto in Eb Major, movement 3, first contrasting episode and rondo theme restatement.

5. The second contrasting episode grows directly out of the restatement of the rondo theme. It is a genuine development section, in which Haydn fragments the rondo theme and treats it to a series of *modulations* (changes of key). **Musical selection:** Haydn, Trumpet Concerto in Eb Major, movement 3, second contrasting episode, rondo theme restatement and conclusion (coda).

Lecture Eight
Beethoven

Scope: The sense of alienation that Ludwig van Beethoven had felt since his unhappy childhood was increased in adulthood by his disastrous love life and the onset of deafness. He was a difficult, generally unhappy man with a chip on his shoulder the size of an old-growth redwood. As a composer, he grew partial to extreme musical contrasts and confrontations, the resolution of which became a vehicle for his personal emotional catharses. The concerto, with its inherent principle of contrast, was an ideal vehicle for Beethoven's self-expression. His belief that expressive content should determine form resulted in an unheard-of degree of formal flexibility. His technical innovations and expressive ideas opened up a whole new world of music. As a child of the Enlightenment, he believed in the integrity of the individual. That belief produced concerti that are metaphors for the individual (the soloist) against the collective (the orchestra). In this lecture, we discuss the Triple Concerto for Violin 'Cello and Piano in C Major, op. 56, of 1803 and Piano Concerto no. 4 in G Major, op. 58, of 1806.

Outline

I. Intellectually, Beethoven (1770–1827) was a child of the Enlightenment, a believer in the primacy of the individual. In Beethoven's hands, the concerto became a metaphor for the inalienable rights and power of the individual.

    A. Increasingly, Beethoven was attracted to extreme musical contrasts. The ultimate resolutions of these confrontations and conflicts became a vehicle for Beethoven's personal emotional catharses, a way for him to face his increasingly silent world as his hearing slowly deteriorated.

    B. Beethoven's increasing use of heightened contrast, conflict, and resolution in his music; his Enlightenment belief in the individual as the essential "unit" in society; his own alienation from society; and his inherent orneriness predisposed him to compose concerti.

  C. His belief in music as an essentially self-expressive art forced him to innovate: He used the time-honored musical forms of both the Classical and the Baroque eras with an unprecedented degree of flexibility, because for him, it was expressive content that determined form, not the other way around. Beethoven was a Classicist but also the first true modernist, a composer whose technical innovations and expressive approach opened the door to an entirely new musical world.

II. Beethoven composed seven concerti: five for piano; one for violin; and one for violin, 'cello, and piano, the Triple Concerto.

  A. The first three piano concerti are considered early works, composed before what is generally considered to be his watershed work, Symphony no. 3 of 1803.

  B. The fourth and fifth piano concerti are the finest of Beethoven's piano concerti, filled with the type of compositional, pianistic, and expressive innovations that changed the course of Western music. Piano Concerto no. 4 in G Major, op. 58, was completed in March 1806, while Piano Concerto no. 5 in Eb Major, op. 73, was completed in 1809, the year Napoleon's army bombarded and occupied Vienna. Because of the war, the concerto's premiere was postponed. It was premiered on February 11, 1812, with Beethoven's student Carl Czerny at the piano, because of Beethoven's growing deafness.

  C. Beethoven composed his Triple Concerto in C Major, op. 56, in 1803 and completed his Violin Concerto in D Major, op. 61, in 1806, the same year as Piano Concerto no. 4. (The Violin Concerto in D Major and the Piano Concerto no. 5 are discussed in detail in Professor Greenberg's Teaching Company course *Concert Masterworks*.) In this lecture, we examine the Triple Concerto as something less than a successful experiment in generic fusion and the Piano Concerto no. 4 as an entirely successful masterwork.

III. In 1802, Beethoven suffered a severe depression over his progressive hearing loss. In 1803, he "reinvented" himself as a hero battling fate, a hero whose sword would be his pen and whose manuscript paper would be the battlefield. His campaigns would seek to plumb the deepest levels of conflict through extreme musical contrasts, and his victories would be the reconciliation of those contrasting and conflicting musical elements. The years 1803–1815 would constitute

Beethoven's "heroic period." The works of 1803 are about something else as well: fusion.

A. Beethoven's works of fusion include his Symphony no. 3, op. 55, which represents a fusion of the symphony with the expressive extremes and dramatic storytelling of the opera house. His Sonata for Violin and Piano, op. 47 (*Kreutzer*), fuses chamber music with the virtuosity of a concerto. The Piano Sonata in C Major, op. 53 (*Waldstein*), fuses the piano sonata with the concerto. Finally, the Triple Concerto for Violin, 'Cello and Piano of 1803 fuses the piano trio (a highly popular genre of chamber music in Beethoven's day) with the concerto.

B. Beethoven's Triple Concerto is not a well-known work. It is also a noble failure. We will examine the Triple Concerto because we can learn as much about Beethoven's methods and priorities from it as we can from Beethoven's successes.

C. The sprawling first movement in double-exposition form is an object lesson in what is not quite right about this work.

  1. Perhaps Beethoven's single greatest compositional skill was his ability to build themes, sections, and entire movements from the most neutral, even banal melodic scraps, by developing them, metamorphosing them, twisting, grafting, recombining, and building them into magnificent palaces of sound, structures that display extraordinary unity and sense of rhetorical flow.

  2. This does not happen in the Triple Concerto, because Beethoven is so focused on allowing each soloist to state the thematic material that there is almost no time for development. As a result, the themes do not transcend their humble beginnings, and their neutral nature cannot withstand the degree of repetition to which they are subjected. Theme 1 of the first movement is a case in point. It is modest to the point of banality. **Musical selection:** Beethoven, Triple Concerto in C Major, op. 56, movement 1, orchestral exposition, theme 1.

  3. In the solo exposition, each soloist, one at a time, enters playing theme 1. **Musical selection:** Beethoven, Triple Concerto in C Major, op. 56, movement 1, solo exposition, theme 1. Although the theme has been embellished, it has not been altered.

4. The development section, which is built almost entirely around theme 1, begins in the same way that the solo exposition did, with each soloist entering playing the theme. A long series of dramatic arpeggios follows. Thematically, they have nothing to do with anything and rather overstay their welcome. **Musical selection:** Beethoven, Triple Concerto in C Major, op. 56, movement 1, development section.

5. The best movement in this work is the third movement, a rondo in which the rondo theme is a polacca (Polish dance, polonaise), one of only three polonaises that Beethoven ever composed. In the movement's conclusion, the meter momentarily shifts from triple to duple. **Musical selection:** Beethoven, Triple Concerto in C Major, op. 56, movement 3, conclusion.

IV. In his indispensable book *The Classical Style*, Charles Rosen makes this point about the convention of double exposition: "The most important fact about [double-exposition form] is that the audience waits for the soloist to enter, and when he stops playing, they wait for him to begin again" (Steinberg, p. 64). This concept is what musicologist Michael Steinberg calls "Rosen's law."

A. Contrary to the convention, in Beethoven's Piano Concerto no. 4, the piano begins the concerto all by itself. The music it plays is anything but soloistic: An exquisitely gentle, chorale-like version of theme 1 establishes the *tonic* (home) key of G major and a lyric, haunting mood. **Musical selection:** Beethoven, Piano Concerto no. 4 in G Major, op. 58, movement 1, orchestral exposition, theme 1.

1. The orchestra responds with a similar phrase but one that begins in the distant key of B major. The effect is incredibly powerful, as if the piano and the orchestra are acknowledging right from the start that although they share thematic material, harmonically, they are of two different worlds. **Musical selection:** Beethoven, Piano Concerto no. 4 in G Major, op. 58, movement 1, orchestral exposition, theme 1.

2. Beethoven has reconciled the piano and orchestra as equals! The soloist does not repeat what the orchestra initially states, but rather, the orchestra repeats what the soloist initially states. All of this is couched in a mood of poetry, mystery, and lyricism that continues to the very end of the final movement.

3. Having established itself as an equal partner, the piano steps aside and lets the orchestra proceed with the remainder of the orchestral exposition. The orchestra expands on theme 1, back in the home key of G major, building it to a powerful climax. **Musical selection:** Beethoven, Piano Concerto no. 4 in G Major, op. 58, movement 1, orchestral exposition, theme 1.
4. Theme 2 begins in A minor but ends in the tonic key of G major. **Musical selection:** Beethoven, Piano Concerto no. 4 in G Major, op. 58, movement 1, orchestral exposition, theme 2.
5. A royal and triumphant cadence follows. **Musical selection:** Beethoven, Piano Concerto no. 4 in G Major, op. 58, movement 1, orchestral exposition, cadence.
6. When Beethoven flew in the face of convention, allowing his soloist to enter at the beginning of the movement, he magnified the tension implied in the second part of that convention: that when the soloist stops playing, the audience awaits his return. Now the anticipation is much greater, because the familiar ground rules no longer apply—who knows when the soloist will return?
7. Just as the cadence material of the orchestral exposition seems about to conclude, the solo piano reenters, bringing the orchestral exposition to a close. Then, with a series of flourishes, scales, and trills, the piano begins the solo exposition. **Musical selection:** Beethoven, Piano Concerto no. 4 in G Major, op. 58, movement 1, piano reentry.
8. Thus, Beethoven retains the large-scale structure of double-exposition form, while allowing the solo piano to come and go as it pleases, with a flexibility that changes the roles and rituals usually observed between the soloist and the ensemble. This exemplifies what is meant by Beethoven's "contextual use of form." He uses traditional musical forms only to the extent that they serve his expressive goals.

B. The solo exposition is double the length of the orchestral exposition, not only because of its extended, virtuosic piano episodes but also because of the introduction of a third theme, in the new key of D major. **Musical selections:** Beethoven, Piano Concerto no. 4 in G Major, op. 58, movement 1, solo exposition, theme 1; theme 3; theme 2; and cadence theme. We should also note that the piano shares these themes with the orchestra. Again, there is tremendous flexibility in Beethoven's approach to the rituals of double-exposition form.

C. The development section begins with a long and increasingly dramatic episode based on the material that the piano played when it entered at the conclusion of the orchestral exposition. **Musical selection:** Beethoven, Piano Concerto no. 4 in G Major, op. 58, movement 1, development, opening.

D. The recapitulation begins with the chorale-like opening of theme 1, now grandly played by the piano. **Musical selection:** Beethoven, Piano Concerto no. 4 in G Major, op. 58, movement 1, recapitulation, opening.

E. Beethoven composed two cadenzas for this first movement: One is relatively easy and was intended for the concerto's dedicatee, Archduke Rudolf; the other is one Beethoven wrote for himself, and it is extremely difficult.

    1. The cadenza Beethoven wrote for himself represents a different sort of piano-writing than anything we heard in the Mozart piano concerti. For one thing, Beethoven's piano was bigger than any piano that Mozart played. But more than that, Beethoven was trained as an organist, and it seems that he wanted from the small, tinny-sounding pianos of his time the same sort of power, sonority, and variety of sound that he could draw from an organ. The pianos of his day, however, were not equal to this particular challenge.

    2. The first-movement cadenza fully displays Beethoven's concept of the piano, with piano-writing that stretches even the resources of the modern concert grand. **Musical selection:** Beethoven, Piano Concerto no. 4 in G Major, op. 58, movement 1, cadenza.

F. The second movement is the famous "lyre of Orpheus" movement, during which the piano "tames" the wild beast that is the orchestra. **Musical selection:** Beethoven, Piano Concerto no. 4 in G Major, op. 58, movement 2, opening. As the movement progresses, the dialogue between lyric piano and the declamatory orchestra increases in intensity, until the piano finally sings such a soulful cadenza that the orchestra is subdued. The ancient idea that music had the power to enlighten, as personified by Orpheus, becomes in

Beethoven's concerto, a symbol of the power of the individual to enlighten and tame the collective.

G. The third-movement rondo finale begins without a pause. For the first time in this work, trumpets and drums are heard, giving the music a wonderfully festive edge. For its lyricism, subtle wit, and spark; crystalline brilliance; and piano virtuosity, there is no finale in the concerto repertoire quite like this one. **Musical selection:** Beethoven, Piano Concerto no. 4 in G Major, op. 58, movement 3, rondo theme, first contrasting episode, rondo theme restatement.

H. Beethoven's Piano Concerto no. 4 received its premiere, with Beethoven at the piano, during the notorious marathon concert of December 22, 1808. This concert also presented the premieres of Beethoven's Symphonies nos. 5 and 6; the Choral Fantasy for Orchestra, Chorus and Piano, op. 80; the Vienna premiere of three movements from Beethoven's Mass in C Major; the concert aria "Ah! Perfido"; and a lengthy improvisation by Beethoven. The concert lasted four hours in a freezing Theater an der Wien, where the heating system had malfunctioned. It is doubtful whether anyone at that concert could have guessed that Beethoven's performance would mark his last as a concerto soloist. After its premiere, Beethoven's Fourth Piano Concerto was not performed again for 20 years.

Lecture Nine
The Romantic Concerto

Scope: In the post-Enlightenment, post-Napoleon, industrial age of the 19th century, the growing middle class had become an economic force to be reckoned with. These *nouveau riche* wanted a cultural experience above and beyond the everyday. They found a response in Romanticism, with its cultivation and celebration of the extreme, including the concept of the artist as hero, a concept that had evolved from the Enlightenment focus on the individual "reveling in his individuality." In the Romantic concerto, it was the soloist who represented the artist as hero, and his vehicle was music designed to showcase his virtuosity as a performer. Indeed, virtuosity, in the words of Franz Liszt, became "an indispensable element of music" (Layton, p. 140). The Romantic focus on virtuosity for its own sake resulted in the predominance of the soloist over the orchestra; the Classical-era partnership between soloist and orchestra took second place to the evolving Romantic ideal. We see this happening in Niccolo Paganini's Violin Concerto no. 1 in D Major. By the time we arrive at Franz Liszt's Piano Concerto no. 1 in Eb Major, even traditional double-exposition form has disappeared in favor of structures that put the "heroic" soloist at the forefront.

Outline

I. Romanticism was a response to the economics and sociology of the 19th century.

    A. Since the early 1790s, the aristocracies across Europe had lost much of their financial and political power, partly because of the ravages of war and partly because of the Enlightenment's vision of a national life based on law and common sense, rather than the arbitrary rule of an aristocratic elite.

    B. By the third decade of the 19th century, the middle class had become the primary economic force in Europe and, as a result, the essential patrons of music. These *nouveau riche* wanted entertainment—spectacle, even titillation, art that plumbed extremes of emotion, including the fantastic and the bizarre.

- **C.** Romanticism answered this need in five ways:
  1. With a celebration of extreme emotions and extreme emotional states.
  2. With a fascination for the grotesque and macabre ("gothick").
  3. With a fascination for nature at its wildest.
  4. With an exploration of nationalism, based on the use of folk or ethnic music in concert music.
  5. With the vision of the artist as hero.
- **D.** The Enlightenment's celebration of individuality placed an idealized member of the middle class at the forefront of society.
  1. The destruction of the French monarchy and subsequent rise of Napoleon shattered the belief that monarchs ruled by divine right and were themselves divine.
  2. Napoleon, like his contemporary Beethoven, was a man of his time, who could not have risen to power without the cultural and political preconditions created by the Enlightenment. Napoleon became the prototype for the post-Enlightenment secular hero, the self-made man, who made himself a success through his own talents, not through a lucky accident of birth.
  3. The Romantic idea of the secular hero—translated into the artist as hero—was particularly influential in Romantic music, where it manifested itself in the concerto.

II. In the concerto, the artist-as-hero idea can be seen in two reinforcing ways: The soloist was increasingly perceived as a luminary, and virtuosity, showcasing the talents of this "luminary," became indispensable.

- **A.** Virtuoso Romantic composer/performers, such as Beethoven, Mozart, and Bach before them, composed music to be performed by themselves.
- **B.** Among the first of these luminaries was the pianist/composer Johann Hummel, a student of Mozart and a rival of Beethoven. His concerti exerted a significant influence on Chopin. (We will discuss Hummel in Lecture Ten.) Other virtuoso concerti composers include Giovanni Battista Viotti (1755–1824); Ignaz Moscheles (1794–1870); Ludwig Spohr (1784–1859); and Carl Maria von Weber (1786–1826).

III. Niccolo Paganini (1782–1840) was a prodigy who practiced 12 hours day. Building on and extending violin techniques as they existed at the time, Paganini became, perhaps, the most technically accomplished violinist of all time. By 1813, he had become a legend in Italy.

A. Among the works Paganini composed to display his incredible technique are six violin concerti. These are not mere technical exercises. Paganini's concerti are filled with beautiful melody and great dramatic timing, classic Italian traits. They also betray the influence of Italian bel canto opera, in particular, the operas of his friend and contemporary Gioacchino Rossini.

B. Paganini's Violin Concerto no. 1 in D Major of 1819 is, structurally, a textbook example of traditional organization: The first movement is in double-exposition form; the second movement is a dramatic and operatic *adagio*; and the third is a brilliant rondo.

  1. The orchestral exposition, which evokes the sound of a contemporary opera overture, has a slow and portentous opening, followed by a brisk, upbeat passage. **Musical selection:** Paganini, Violin Concerto no. 1 in D Major, movement 1, orchestral exposition, theme 1. This marks both the first and the last time in this concerto that the orchestra will play for any appreciable length of time by itself.

  2. The solo exposition makes it clear that this concerto is not a partnership in the Classical sense. Everything is secondary to the solo violin, with its transcendental virtuosity. **Musical selection:** Paganini, Violin Concerto no. 1 in D Major, movement 1, solo exposition, theme 1.

C. The second movement fully exploits the violin's capacity to sing. **Musical selection:** Paganini, Violin Concerto no. 1 in D Major, movement 2, opening.

D. The third-movement rondo is a virtuosic tour-de-force for the violin. The rondo theme demands one of Paganini's favorite techniques: "ricochet" bowing, in which the bow is made to bounce up and down the strings, creating a fast, staccato effect. The "ricochet" bowing alternates with extremely high notes that must be played on the violin's E string. This is the most "difficult to tame" of the violin's four strings. **Musical selection:** Paganini, Violin Concerto no. 1 in D Major, movement 3, opening.

1. Paganini's virtuosity baffled his audiences, and they created outlandish explanations for it, including the notion that his violin's E string was made from the intestine of a mistress he had murdered.
2. The first contrasting episode of the third-movement rondo features the violin playing double stops (multiple simultaneous notes) and rapid figurations at the very top of the instrument. For all its incredible pyrotechnics, however, this music still makes sense as a composition. **Musical selection:** Paganini, Violin Concerto no. 1 in D Major, movement 3, first contrasting episode.
3. This sort of violin playing had never been heard before, and Paganini took care to protect his technical innovations from competition by refusing to publish them. As a result, his first two concerti were not published until 1851, and nos. 3–6 were not published until the 1970s.

E. In the words of musicologist Boris Schwartz, writing in the *New Grove Dictionary of Music and Musicians*, Paganini's "tone had infinite shadings…he displayed a phenomenal command of the fingerboard. His double stops and chords showed infinite variety."

IV. Paganini had a major impact on succeeding generations of violinists and on a pianist, as well—the 21-year-old Franz Liszt (1811–1886).

A. When he heard Paganini play at the Paris Opera House in April 1832, Liszt decided that his mission was to become the "Paganini of the piano."

B. At that time, Liszt was already a formidable pianist, who had studied piano with Beethoven's student Carl Czerny and composition with Antonio Salieri. After he heard Paganini play, Liszt spent the next 15 years practicing relentlessly and working on every conceivable challenge in piano playing.

C. Liszt was defining what was possible on an instrument that was only just coming into existence—the modern piano emerged from the Paris workshops of Pleyel and Erard in the 1830s and 1840s.

D. Liszt turned himself into one of the greatest showmen who ever lived.

E. He composed two piano concerti, beginning the first in the early 1830s and continuing to revise it as late as 1853. This concerto, in

Eb major, is a perfect example of Liszt's unconventionality. Liszt believed that form must follow content.

F. Piano Concerto no. 1 in Eb Major has four movements, of which movements 2–4 are played without pause. They are united through a cyclical use of themes.

1. Double exposition has no place in Liszt's first movement. The predominance of the orchestra in the orchestral exposition goes against Liszt's image of the dominant "virtuoso hero." Instead, he adapted sonata form to follow his conviction that form must follow expressive content and to reflect his concept of piano (and pianist) as hero.

2. In the first movement, the strings, punctuated by brass and winds, intone a chromatically descending, dark and dramatic theme 1. **Musical selection:** Liszt, Piano Concerto no. 1 in Eb Major, movement 1, theme 1.

3. The orchestra has the floor for only 13 seconds (four measures) before the overwhelming dominance of the piano becomes apparent, with two massive rising fanfares in octaves, accompanied recitative-like by the orchestra. **Musical selection:** Liszt, Piano Concerto no. 1 in Eb Major, movement 1, theme 1, piano entry.

4. In this concerto, the orchestra is reduced to the role of an accompanist. The piano makes this clear with three cadenzas in the first movement, the first of which expands on the descending chromatic element of theme 1 before embarking on a smooth, rising scale. **Musical selection:** Liszt, Piano Concerto no. 1 in Eb Major, movement 1, theme 1, cadenza.

5. The orchestra briefly plays the opening of theme 1. **Musical selection:** Liszt, Piano Concerto no. 1 in Eb Major, movement 1, theme 1 (measures 27–29).

6. The piano returns to play a lyric episode. **Musical selection:** Liszt, Piano Concerto no. 1 in Eb Major, movement 1, lyric episode (measures 30–33).

7. The orchestra briefly reasserts the opening of theme 1. **Musical selection:** Liszt, Piano Concerto no. 1 in Eb Major, movement 1, theme 1, opening (measure 34).

8. A second piano cadenza follows that combines the magnificence of theme 1 with the gentleness of the lyric episode; a solo clarinet joins the piano in a melancholy duet

about halfway through this cadenza. **Musical selection:** Liszt, Piano Concerto no. 1 in Eb Major, movement 1, cadenza.

9. The second cadenza turns into theme 2, a wistful, descending theme closely related to the opening of theme 1. The setting is chamber-like in its delicacy, as first a clarinet, then violins, then a gradually increasing number of instruments join the piano, as it builds to a climax marked *appassionato* (passionately). **Musical selection:** Liszt, Piano Concerto no. 1 in Eb Major, movement 1, theme 2.

10. In the cadence material, the full orchestra proclaims theme 1, followed by a series of rising octaves in the piano. **Musical selection:** Liszt, Piano Concerto no. 1 in Eb Major, movement 1, cadence material.

G. The development section is divided into two brief episodes. In the first, the piano plays huge, roaring, descending octaves based on the opening of theme 1, accompanied by the orchestra. In the second episode, scored for piano alone, the piano plays a majestic chordal fanfare drawn from its entry at measure 5. **Musical selection:** Liszt, Piano Concerto no. 1 in Eb Major, movement 1, development section.

H. Next comes a recapitulation of sorts, in which the orchestra and piano alternate, respectively, the opening of theme 1 and the lyric episode. The recapitulation concludes with the third and final piano cadenza: a brief episode, rippling downward and leading to the coda. **Musical selection:** Liszt, Piano Concerto no. 1 in Eb Major, movement 1, recapitulation.

I. The coda consists of a gentle version of the opening of theme 1, played by the orchestra and accompanied by rippling arpeggios in the piano—the first and only time in this movement that the piano accompanies the orchestra.

J. Liszt's ingenious innovations as a pianistic pioneer, as an interpreter of other's composers' music, and as a music aesthetician profoundly influenced generations of composers, including his friend Hector Berlioz and his son-in-law Richard Wagner. As a composer, however, he was frequently a little too reactive. In the coda for this movement, the piano accompanies the orchestra, despite the fact that this is totally out of character with everything that has preceded it. **Musical selection:** Liszt, Piano Concerto no. 1 in Eb Major, movement 1, coda.

K. Liszt was the secular hero of his time, whose persona and music exemplified the most extreme aspects of Romanticism. His music spoke to many in the 19th century as the music of the future.

Lecture Ten
Hummel and Chopin

Scope: Polish-born Frederick Chopin considered his compositional style to have evolved directly from Mozart. Chopin's link to Mozart was Johann Nepomuk Hummel, who had studied with Mozart. Hummel's piano concerti are well crafted in the Classical style, though Hummel's pianism goes far beyond its Mozartean roots in its Romantic virtuosity. Chopin was impressed by Hummel's virtuosic piano playing and by the stylish, post-Classical music that Hummel composed. Hummel's Piano Concerto in A Minor and the Piano Concerto in B Minor (which is discussed in this lecture) were essential influences on Chopin. Paradoxically, Chopin embraced the Romantic revolutionary mindset while professing to detest Romanticism. He was an innovator in his amazing harmonic palette and his extraordinary pianism. Of his two piano concerti, Piano Concerto no. 2 in F Minor, op. 21, is discussed in this lecture. It exhibits elements that became hallmarks of his mature style, including his use of Polish dance rhythms, melodies with a somewhat Slavic flavor, extraordinary rhythmic flexibility, bel canto lyric sensibility, and a pianism like no other.

Outline

I. Frederick Chopin (1810–1849) is that rarest of composers whose music is as beloved and respected today as it was when it was first performed. Johann Nepomuk Hummel (1778–1837), on the other hand, is better known as a student of Mozart and rival of Beethoven than as a composer in his own right. In Hummel's case, history has not been fair.

    A. Hummel's pianistic influence on Chopin was a decisive element in Chopin's development. When Chopin first heard Hummel play the piano in Warsaw in 1828, he was astounded by Hummel's virtuosity and his music, which Chopin perceived to be modern without suffering from a lack of elegance or expressive overkill.

    B. Despite his innovative treatment of the piano and his completely "modern" expressive, harmonic, and melodic palette, Chopin believed he had evolved directly from Mozart—not from

Beethoven and certainly not from the Romantics, whose music he detested. Chopin's link to Mozart was through Hummel.

II. Hummel was a child prodigy violinist *and* pianist. At the age of seven, in 1785, he played piano for Mozart, who was so impressed that he gave Hummel daily piano lessons free of charge. Through Mozart, Hummel met and performed for the Viennese aristocracy. Piano lessons with Muzio Clementi, organ lessons with Joseph Haydn, vocal composition lessons with Antonio Salieri, and even a few piano lessons with Beethoven followed, giving Hummel one of the best pedigrees in the history of Western music.

- **A.** Hummel's style of piano playing and improvising descended directly from the Mozartean ideal of clarity, elegant melody, and artistic restraint. To this, Hummel added a considerable degree of virtuosity for its own sake. He was the last of the great Viennese pianists in his preference for light, not-very-sonorous Viennese pianos, as opposed to the English and French pianos favored by Liszt and Chopin and their successors.
- **B.** As a composer, Hummel is underrated today. He wrote eight piano concerti, a mandolin concerto, a double concerto for violin and piano, and a trumpet concerto, which is the most frequently performed of Hummel's concerti.
- **C.** The best known of Hummel's piano concerti is the Piano Concerto in B Minor, op. 89, of 1819. It is Classical in structure: a double-exposition first movement; a slow, lyric second movement; and a third-movement rondo. The latter is a spectacularly virtuoso movement, with a brief introduction that leads directly to a brilliant, Hungarian-tinted rondo theme, presented by the piano. **Musical selection:** Hummel, Piano Concerto in B Minor, op. 89, movement 3, introduction and rondo theme.
    - **1.** The first contrasting episode begins with a dramatic orchestral passage, during which the piano takes a break from the first two virtuoso movements and prepares for what follows—a passage of 3 minutes and 50 seconds in duration, during which the piano soloist plays, non-stop, some of the most difficult music imaginable. It is mostly "finger" music, consisting of scales and arpeggios in the style of Classical pianism, rather than "arm" music that features huge leaps and thundering sonorities. It is a minefield of technical treachery:

A lengthy piano episode leads to a chipper, memorable, trill-dominated contrasting theme that will be developed and followed by the first restatement of the rondo theme—and all of it played by the piano. **Musical selection:** Hummel, Piano Concerto in B Minor, op. 89, movement 3, first contrasting episode and rondo theme restatement.
2. We should stand in awe of the steel-fingered modern pianist who is willing and able to play this piano part, because this music was conceived for the light-actioned Viennese pianos of the 1810s, not the huge, much heavier modern piano, on which this music is much more difficult to play.
3. The coda that concludes this third and final movement features finger-oriented, Classically-based, Mozart-inspired pianism that, nevertheless, embraces a degree of Romantic virtuosity, putting it far beyond its model. **Musical selection:** Hummel, Piano Concerto in B Minor, op. 89, movement 3, coda.

D. The current view of Hummel's music as decorative, "chandelier" music is much too harsh. The problem with the Piano Concerto in B Minor is not the music but the fact that no one is willing to perform it, especially on a modern piano. It is just too hard to play, and the rewards offered by such a piece are not perceived as being equal to the time required to learn it and the risks involved in its performance. This is an unfortunate fate for some first-class piano concerti.

III. Frederic Chopin's music and his attitude toward music represent a paradox.

A. Chopin was a genuinely revolutionary composer, whose harmonic usage was so subtle and advanced that he was accused of writing music that was "earsplittingly dissonant, inexplicable, perhaps insane."
1. He, along with Franz Liszt, defined the capabilities of the new piano technology, particularly in terms of expressive nuance and the range of sounds and sonorities that could be drawn from the new metal-harped pianos. His use of rhythm, particularly *rubato*, was also revolutionary, and he would seem to have been an arch-Romantic in terms of the

otherworldly expressive content and effortless, lyric "spontaneity" of his music.

    2. Yet, paradoxically, Chopin professed to hate Romanticism. He believed that the word *Romantic* was a preemptive apologia for artistic tastelessness; he disliked Romantic visual art; he was physically sickened by the music of Hector Berlioz; he claimed that Liszt's music was utterly empty of real meaning; and he disparaged the music of Robert Schumann, despite the fact that it was Schumann who put Chopin on the musical map. (Schumann wrote a glowing review of Chopin's Variations on Mozart's *La ci darem la mano*, the same review that contains the famous line "Hats off gentlemen, a genius!") Chopin ignored the music of Mendelssohn and Schubert and found Beethoven's music to be in poor taste. The only composers he claimed to like were Johann Sebastian Bach, Wolfgang Mozart, and his contemporary, Vincenzo Bellini.

B. Chopin was born in Warsaw, Poland, in 1810 to a Polish mother and French father. By his teens, he had become a celebrity in Warsaw, and he enjoyed socializing with Warsaw's elite. He acquired a *hauteur* and a love for the finest things that society could offer, qualities that gained him almost instant entry to the highest circles of society when he relocated to Paris in 1831.

C. He had composed two piano concerti between 1829 and 1830, which he intended for his entry into the musical circles of Western Europe. The essential influences on these concerti were Hummel's Piano Concerti in A Minor and B Minor and concerti by Ignaz Moscheles and John Field. Typical of his models and the "heroic" concerti of the time, Chopin's piano concerti are showpieces for the piano that treat the orchestra as an accompanist, not as a partner.

D. Chopin's piano concerti are early works written before his exposure to Liszt, Berlioz, Beethoven, Mendelssohn, and all the other composers he professed to dislike, but from whom he stole when it suited him. From the time he arrived in Paris to the end of his life 18 years later, he devoted himself exclusively to writing solo piano music.

E. Chopin's two piano concerti are numbered in reverse order. His Piano Concerto in F Minor was the first to be composed but is now identified as no. 2 because it was published after the Piano Concerto in E Minor, which is known as no. 1. In my opinion, the F minor work is the better of the two: more compact and more dramatically compelling.

F. The first movement double-exposition form is the most pedantic, least "Chopin-like" movement in the concerto. The orchestral exposition presents themes that sound colorless when played by the orchestra but are multi-hued when played by the piano. This is due to more than orchestration. Perhaps more than any other composer in the history of Western music, Chopin spoke through the piano. The music he wrote for orchestra is, at its basic level, piano music, and it sounds fully realized only when it is played on the piano. This quality is exemplified by the first theme of the orchestral exposition. **Musical selection:** Chopin, Piano Concerto no. 2 in F Minor, op. 21, movement 1, orchestral exposition, theme 1.

  1. When the piano plays this music at the beginning of the solo exposition, it sounds like a different theme entirely. By using the entire keyboard, by embellishing the theme very slightly, and by allowing the piano part a degree of rhythmic flexibility that he cannot allow the orchestra, Chopin breathes life into this theme. It becomes just that exquisite sort of melancholy, lyric theme for which Chopin was deservedly famous. **Musical selection:** Chopin, Piano Concerto no. 2 in F Minor, op. 21, movement 1, solo exposition, theme 1. Chopin conceived this theme at the piano, then arranged it for orchestra in order to fulfill the requirements of double-exposition form. As orchestra music, it loses almost entirely its spontaneity, wistful melancholy, and lyric grace.

  2. The same thing can be said of theme 2. **Musical selection:** Chopin, Piano Concerto no. 2 in F Minor, op. 21, movement 1, orchestral exposition, theme 2.

  3. When the piano plays this theme, it is transformed from lint to the purest silk. **Musical selection:** Chopin, Piano Concerto no. 2 in F Minor, op. 21, movement 1, solo exposition, theme 2.

  4. The concerto comes into its own in the second and third movements. Here, Chopin is free of the necessity to follow the formal line of double-exposition form and can do what he pleases—that is, turn the concerto over to the piano.

G. The second movement (*larghetto*) is a magnificent example of what would come to be called in Chopin's mature music the technique of *ornamental melody*. Chopin's melodic lines are ornamental by their very nature. The piano presents a highly ornamented, nuanced melody that seemingly has no end. It is supported by an incredibly subtle and complex harmonic accompaniment. Structurally, the second movement is a simple three-part form (A–B–A^1) with a brief orchestral introduction and coda. Chopin's liquid melodic and harmonic fluency is unprecedented. **Musical selection:** Chopin, Piano Concerto no. 2 in F Minor, op. 21, movement 2, opening.

H. The virtuosity of Chopin's writing is incidental, rather than intrinsic, to the piano part—everything the piano plays serves a musical end. We first notice the beauty of the music, rather than how difficult it might be to play.

I. The spectacular third movement is a mazurka gone wild. A mazurka is a Polish dance in triple meter and moderate tempo, in which an accent generally falls on the third beat of each metric unit: ‖: 1–2–**3** :‖. Like Chopin's mazurkas for solo piano, this mazurka has a fairly straightforward three-part form (A–B–A^1) with a coda/finale.

  1. As Chopin's career progressed, he increasingly cultivated such three-part forms. Ultimately, the simplicity of the movement's large-scale form is not the point. What matters is Chopin's achingly beautiful thematic material, his subtle but constant process of thematic development, his amazing harmonic palette, and his extraordinarily original use of the keyboard.

  2. The first theme of the third movement is a folk-inspired mazurka. **Musical selection:** Chopin, Piano Concerto no. 2 in F Minor, op. 21, movement 3, theme A.

  3. According to John Rink of the University of London, this opening was probably inspired by the third movement of Hummel's Piano Concerto in A Minor, op. 85. **Musical selection:** Hummel, Piano Concerto in A Minor, op. 85, movement 3, opening.

4. The central B section of the third movement of Chopin's Piano Concerto in F Minor sees the introduction of a new mazurka tune in Ab major, accompanied by strumming, almost guitar-like strings. **Musical selection:** Chopin, Piano Concerto no. 2 in F Minor, op. 21, movement 3, theme B.

5. The coda/finale presents some of the most brilliant piano writing in the entire concerto. It is more than just a coda: Chopin introduces a number of new piano figures (if not new themes) and an entirely new key as well—F major—in which the concerto concludes. The coda/finale begins quietly with a horn call based on the opening of theme B. From there, the piano plays almost continuously through the explosive conclusion of the movement. **Musical selection:** Chopin, Piano Concerto no. 2 in F Minor, op. 21, movement 3, finale.

J. No works of Chopin have received more negative criticism than his two piano concerti. For example, critics have argued that Chopin's use of the orchestra is ineffective and his handling of double exposition is stiff. We could keep in mind, however, that these concerti are the work of a young composer. They display all those elements that would become hallmarks of Chopin's mature style: his use of Polish dance rhythms and vaguely Slavi-sounding melodies, extraordinary rhythmic flexibility, genuinely bel canto lyric sensibility, and a pianism unlike any other. These concerti went a long way toward establishing Chopin as a major talent, and whatever their flaws, they represent a composer whose music we cannot live without.

Lecture Eleven
Mendelssohn and Schumann

Scope: Felix Mendelssohn was an outstanding pianist, with a perfect ear and an incredible musical memory. His compositional style was relatively conservative, and he was a master of Classical balance. In his Violin Concerto in E Minor of 1844, for example, he treats the orchestra as a genuine partner with the solo instrument. His solo part is virtuosic but not to the excesses so prevalent in his day. For all his relative conservatism, however, Mendelssohn was a structural innovator who used sonata form instead of double-exposition form in the first movements of his concerti and pioneered the idea of placing the cadenza at the end of the development section, rather than at the end of the recapitulation. Robert Schumann, who revered Mendelssohn, was a genuine Romantic who believed that music should express the personal and the self-revelationary. Yet his music is profoundly influenced by Beethoven, Bach, Mozart, and the Italian school. His 'Cello Concerto in A Minor of 1850 brings soloist and orchestra together in a symphonic approach to the genre. The work became a model and inspiration for Antonin Dvorak's transcendental 'cello concerto of 1895.

Outline

I. Mendelssohn and Schumann are frequently paired in music surveys and textbooks. Yet Mendelssohn, although he liked Robert Schumann personally, found his music distasteful. Schumann, on the other hand, considered Mendelssohn to be the preeminent musician of his day.

   A. Felix Mendelssohn (1809–1847) was one of the greatest child prodigies in the history of Western music. He grew up in a wealthy Jewish family that believed that assimilation and acceptance were the keys to survival. He was a superb pianist with a perfect ear and a freakish musical memory. As a child, he memorized all of Beethoven's symphonies and could play them on the piano.

   B. Despite his ability to play difficult music, Mendelssohn did not indulge in virtuosic display, nor did he compose music that celebrated the virtuoso as hero above all else. His concerti, like the great bulk of his music, reflect a certain Classical conservatism in their expressive and compositional content. He was adventurous but not an over-the-top Romantic.

    C. Mendelssohn composed eight concerti, of which three are mature works: the Piano Concerto in G Minor, op. 25 (1831); the Piano Concerto in D Minor, op. 40 (1837); and the Violin Concerto in E minor, op. 64 (1844).

II. Mendelssohn's mature style, which displays a Mozartean refinement, informed but not overpowered by a certain post-Beethoven, Romantic expressive impulse, is perfectly demonstrated in his concerti. The sort of pianism we hear in these concerti draws more from Hummel than from Mendelssohn's contemporaries, Liszt, Chopin, or Schumann.

    A. Though relatively conservative, Mendelssohn was responsible for an innovation that became the standard in the 19th-century concerto from Liszt to Brahms and beyond. Rather than use double-exposition form in his first movements, he used a streamlined version of sonata form: The movement begins with the solo exposition and moves directly on to the development section. This made sense in the "era of the soloist," when a lengthy orchestral exposition had become essentially irrelevant to the dramatic substance of the concerto.

    B. The first movement of Mendelssohn's Piano Concerto in G Minor, op. 25 (1831), opens with a brief, dramatic introduction played by the orchestra, followed immediately by theme 1 played by the piano. This is not easy piano music to play, but neither is it an example of the sort of virtuosity for its own sake that we hear in Listz's piano concerti. **Musical selection:** Mendelssohn, Piano Concerto in G Minor, op. 25, movement 1, theme 1.

    C. After this, the orchestra plays a dramatic and extended modulating bridge, before the piano returns to play the lyric and quiet theme 2. The role of the orchestra is reduced in comparison to Classical-era models, but the orchestra is not the mere shadow of its former self that it is in Liszt's Piano Concerto in Eb Major.

III. In 1842, Mendelssohn founded a school of music in Leipzig, where he held the position of music director of the prestigious Gewandhaus Orchestra. Given Mendelssohn's celebrity and the eminent faculty he

assembled, the Leipzig Conservatory quickly became one of the most renowned schools of its kind in the world.
- **A.** Among the conservatory's first students was a 12-year-old violin prodigy named Joseph Joachim, who became Mendelssohn's protégé. Joachim's violin teacher was Ferdinand David, a close friend of Mendelssohn, for whom Mendelssohn wrote a violin concerto.
- **B.** The Violin Concerto in E Minor was premiered at the Leipzig Gewandhaus on March 13, 1845, with Ferdinand David as soloist, under the baton of Mendelssohn's friend and colleague Niels Gade. Sitting in the audience was Joseph Joachim, who would perform the concerto more than 200 times. The concerto's three movements are played without pause.
- **C.** Mendelssohn reveals his Classical leanings in the first movement of the concerto by his sense of balance: The solo violin displays a perfect balance between the sort of virtuosity to be expected from a concerto composed in 1844 and pure lyricism; Mendelssohn treats the orchestra as a key element in the musical drama, balancing the soloist with the ensemble—a balance that is foreign to the concerti of Paganini, Liszt, Hummel, and even Chopin.
    - **1.** Theme 1 is a case in point. The movement begins with the briefest of orchestral introductions; the solo violin enters and plays one of the most elegant, heartrending tunes in the repertoire high on its E string. The orchestra then plays its own version of the theme. **Musical selection:** Mendelssohn, Violin Concerto in E Minor, op. 64, movement 1, theme 1.
    - **2.** The modulating bridge begins with a transition theme, first played by the orchestra, after which it is expanded by the solo violin. Again, this is an example of Mendelssohn's sense of balance. **Musical selection:** Mendelssohn, Violin Concerto in E Minor, op. 64, movement 1, transition and modulating bridge.
    - **3.** A sense of balance is again evident in theme 2, an achingly lyric theme in the new key of G major, which emerges in the winds, accompanied by a sustained low G on the solo violin (the violin's lowest note). Eventually, the solo violin takes over and brilliantly leads the exposition to its conclusion. **Musical selection:** Mendelssohn, Violin Concerto in E Minor, op. 64, movement 1, theme 2 and exposition conclusion.

D. The development section features another of Mendelssohn's innovations: Rather than place the cadenza in the recapitulation, just before the end of the movement, Mendelssohn puts it at the end of the development section. This is effective for several reasons:
   1. It avoids the portentous run-up to the cadenza through the cadential six-four chord, which had become a hackneyed cliché by 1844.
   2. It gives the cadenza a structural, rather than a merely decorative, role by allowing it to pave the way for the recapitulation.
   3. The movement can now conclude with a dramatic bang, uninterrupted by the otherwise predictable appearance of the cadenza.
   4. In one of the most magical moments, the cadenza's conclusion overlaps with the beginning of the recapitulation, as the orchestra enters with theme 1. **Musical selection:** Mendelssohn, Violin Concerto in E Minor, op. 64, movement 1, cadenza and recapitulation opening.

E. The second movement (*andante*) in C major is a hauntingly beautiful and passionate song without words.

F. The third movement, in E major, features the sort of spry, elfin music for which the adjective *Mendelssohnian* was created. The second and third movements are connected by a wistful interlude, or *intermezzo*. **Musical selections:** Mendelssohn, Violin Concerto in E Minor, op. 64, movement 2, interlude, and movement 3, opening.

G. Mendelssohn was a compositional conservative with a respect for the forms and conventions of both the Classical and the Baroque eras. But he could shock his audiences with his structural innovations, and although he was largely immune to the "artist as God" mentality so fashionable during his career, he used aspects of Romanticism when they served his expressive needs.

IV. Robert Schumann (1810–1856) was awed by Mendelssohn. When Liszt once praised the composer Giacomo Meyerbeer at Mendelssohn's expense, Schumann was furious, and the scene he made became a famous anecdote.

A. Schumann composed piano music, songs, symphonies, cantatas, and chamber music. His budding career as a pianist was cut short when he injured his hand by over-practicing. His life was cut short by tertiary syphilis at the age of 46. He was the father of seven children and the husband of Clara Schumann, the most famous female pianist of her time.

B. In terms of his compositional style, Schumann combined the muscular expressivity of Beethoven, the complex polyphony and spirituality of his fellow Lutheran Johann Sebastian Bach, and the lyricism of Mozart and the Italian school with a genuinely Romantic belief that music was a vehicle for the most profound personal confession and self-revelation.

C. Schumann composed three concerti: the Piano Concerto in A Minor, op. 54, of 1845; the 'Cello Concerto in A Minor, op. 129, of 1850; and the Violin Concerto in D Minor of 1853.

D. The violin concerto, written not long before Schumann was institutionalized in an insane asylum, was considered by its dedicatee, Joseph Joachim, to be a discredit to its composer. Joachim hid the manuscript and willed it to the Prussian State Library in Berlin, with the stipulation that it not be published until 1956. It was forgotten until 1937, when it was published and performed.

E. While Schumann's piano music is not easy to play, it does not display the kind of virtuosity for its own sake so prevalent in his day. It is a singularly poetic and intensely personal body of music.

F. Schumann's piano concerto began its life in 1841 as a one-movement work entitled Concert-Allegro for Piano and Orchestra. By 1845, frustrated by his inability to get the piece performed or published, Schumann decided to turn it into a three-movement piano concerto.

G. Schumann brought a symphonic approach to the concerto. The piano and orchestra are equal partners in the sort of abstract thematic exploration and development that we typically associate with the genre of symphony rather than the more theatrical genre of concerto. In the first-movement sonata form, the piano soloist and the orchestra are in perfect balance; the theme itself is a gentle, melancholy chorale that has everything to do with lyricism and mood and virtually nothing to do with virtuosity per se. **Musical**

selection: Schumann, Piano Concerto in A Minor, op. 54, movement 1, theme 1.

H. The second movement is a sweet but entirely unsentimental essay of chamber-music-like proportions, and the third movement is a virtuosic *allegro vivace*, in which the virtuosity is always in the service of the music. This is a wonderful and justly popular concerto.

I. Schumann's 'Cello Concerto in A Minor, op. 129 of 1850, and Saint-Saens' 'Cello Concerto in A Minor of 1873 were the only important 'cello concerti between that of Haydn in 1871 and that of Dvorak in 1895.

J. Why are there so few 19th-century 'cello concerti? Orchestral balance is difficult to achieve in a 'cello concerto, because a solo 'cello is easily drowned out by the orchestra. The orchestra must be used sparingly, something antithetical to the grand, expressive imaginations of the arch-Romantics and the audiences that consumed their music.

K. It is telling that the great 19th-century 'cello concerti—Schumann's, Saint-Saens', and Dvorak's—were written by anti-virtuosi, composers for whom genuine musical content was much more important than virtuosic display.

L. The first theme that begins the first movement of Schumann's 'Cello Concerto in A Minor is achingly lyric. Quiet winds and murmuring strings introduce the 'cello, which is then accompanied by the most thinly scored of orchestral strings. The entire orchestra will enter only at the very end of the excerpt and only then when the 'cello is not actually playing. **Musical selection:** Schumann, 'Cello Concerto in A Minor, op. 129, movement 1, theme 1.

M. The slow second movement has the quality of a song, and the hushed winds and predominantly plucked string accompaniment give it a genuinely chamber-music-like sensibility. **Musical selection:** Schumann, 'Cello Concerto in A Minor, op. 129, movement 2, opening.

N. The three movements of this concerto are played without pause. As in Mendelssohn's violin concerto, Schumann provides an intermezzo between the second and third movements. The intermezzo amounts to a thematic review of the concerto to this point. The intermezzo begins with a woodwind choir, then the 'cello playing a version of theme 1 from the first movement. **Musical selection:** Schumann, 'Cello Concerto in A Minor, op. 129, intermezzo.

1. The music slows as the 'cello now plays the opening of the second movement. **Musical selection:** Schumann, 'Cello Concerto in A Minor, op. 129, intermezzo.
2. Then faster, tremolo strings and downward-swooping winds accompany a recitative-like line in the solo 'cello, which breaking free of the orchestra, speeds up, descends, and moves directly into the third and final movement. **Musical selection:** Schumann, 'Cello Concerto in A Minor, op. 129, intermezzo, conclusion, and movement 3, opening.

O. This concerto became a model and inspiration for Antonin Dvorak's 'cello concerto, simply the greatest 'cello concerto ever written, a piece we will examine in Lecture Fifteen.

Lecture Twelve
Romantic Masters

Scope: In this lecture, we discuss the work of seven Romantic composers, beginning with Henri Vieuxtemps, whose Violin Concerto in F# Minor is a great virtuoso work, written by a teenager, that shows an outstanding grasp of the orchestra and musical structure. The violin pyrotechnics of this concerto are equalled by those of Henryk Wieniawski's Violin Concerto no. 2 in D Minor, which is also characterized by Slavic-sounding melodies, inspired by Wieniawski's native Poland. Max Bruch's Violin Concerto in G Minor has been described by the violinist Joseph Joachim as being the "richest" and "most seductive" of German violin concerti. Bruch's contribution to the genre is notable for music that is supremely suited to the lyric capabilities of the violin. Edvard Grieg's Piano Concerto in A Minor was modeled on Robert Schumann's piano concerto, though its solo part is Lisztian in its virtuosity, and the influence of Grieg's native Norwegian folk music is evident, particularly in the third-movement finale. Moritz Moszkowski's Piano Concerto in E Major and Ignaz Paderewski's Piano Concerto in A Minor are two 19th-century concerti that have been unjustly neglected over the years. Moszkowski's four-movement concerto is notable for its brilliant pianism and sparkling, memorable themes; Paderewski's concerto is equally virtuosic and features highly stylized Polish dance rhythms. Finally, we come to two concerti by Richard Strauss: his Horn Concerto no. 1 of 1883 and his Oboe Concerto in D Major of 1945—two brilliant works that reveal Struass's compositional voice at the antipodes of his career.

Outline

I. In this lecture, we look at seven Romantic concerti that we can expect to hear performed from time to time or that deserve to be heard more often. They were composed by Henri Vieuxtemps, Max Bruch, Edvard Grieg, Moritz Moszkowski, Ignaz Paderewski, and Richard Strauss.

    A. Henri Vieuxtemps (1820–1881) was a Belgian-born violin prodigy who gave his first concert at the age of 6 in his hometown of

Verviers. In 1833, he went to Vienna and studied counterpoint with Simon Sechter, who also taught Franz Schubert and Anton Bruckner. In 1834, he was called the "next Paganini" by Robert Schumann, and in the same year, Paganini himself predicted a brilliant future for the 14-year-old *wunderkind*.

B. Vieuxtemps spent the winter of 1835–1836 in Paris, where he studied composition with Anton Reicha. The major fruit of this study was the Violin Concerto in F# Minor. Although this was Vieuxtemps' first concerto, it was the second to be published and is, therefore, known as no. 2.

 1. This is a great virtuoso concerto. The 16-year-old Vieuxtemps' handling of the orchestra is outstanding, as is his grasp of musical structure. The first movement is a well-wrought double-exposition form, the second movement is a brief but lovely andante, and the third movement is a knockout rondo.
 2. In the third-movement rondo, following a dramatic orchestral introduction, the solo violin plays the rondo theme: a Hungarian-tinted dance tune in the style of Liszt, played high on the violin's E string in the style of Paganini. **Musical selection:** Vieuxtemps, Violin Concerto no. 2 in F# Minor, op. 19, movement 3, rondo theme.
 3. As the rondo unfolds, the violin pyrotechnics multiply, including a group of 52 staccato notes that must be played in just one movement of the bow and a spectacular cadenza. At the end of the movement, after the final return of the rondo theme, the violin plays a series of octaves, followed by an explosive group of quadruple stops—four-note chords—as the concerto comes to its conclusion. **Musical selection:** Vieuxtemps, Violin Concerto no. 2 in F# Minor, op. 19, movement 3, conclusion.

C. Vieuxtemps composed nine concerti, seven for violin and two for 'cello. They remained a cornerstone of the repertoire through the 19th century, particularly in France.

II. Henryk Wieniawski (1835–1880) was, after Paganini, the greatest violinist of the 19th century. He was also an excellent composer who combined the pyrotechnics of Paganini with a Romantic expressive impulse, colored by a Slavic melodic sensibility, inspired by his native Poland.

- **A.** Wieniawski composed two violin concerti, the second of which, composed in 1862, remains a standard of the repertoire to this day. It was premiered in 1862 at the St. Petersburg Conservatory under the baton of Anton Rubinstein. In the audience that night was the Russian composer and music critic Cesar Cui, who was known for writing nasty reviews. He was swept away by the concerto, particularly by its Polish musical nationalism, the same sort of Slavic nationalism that Cui was passionately advocating in Russian music circles.

- **B.** The third and final movement of the concerto is a rondo marked "moderately fast, in gypsy style." The introduction is followed by some high-energy gypsy fiddling. **Musical selection:** Wieniawski, Violin Concerto no. 2 in D Minor, op. 22, movement 3, introduction and rondo theme.

- **C.** Wieniawski saves some of his best violin pyrotechnics for the conclusion of the movement. We begin with a long trill at the very highest reaches of the violin, followed first by the rondo theme, then by a genuinely gypsy-sounding tune—theme B of the rondo—followed by the conclusion of the movement. The music strikes a balance between spectacle and real musical substance. **Musical selection:** Wieniawski, Violin Concerto no. 2 in D Minor, op. 22, movement 3, conclusion.

III. At his 75th birthday in 1906, the great violinist Joseph Joachim listed what he considered the greatest of the German violin concerti: those of Beethoven, Brahms, Mendelssohn, and Bruch. He called Bruch's the "richest" and "most seductive."

- **A.** Max Bruch's violin concerto has been a mainstay of the repertoire since its premiere on April 24, 1866. Bruch (1838–1920) was a conservative composer, and this conservatism is reflected in his treatment of the violin as a bel canto voice.

- **B.** Bruch labeled the first movement of his Violin Concerto in G Minor, op. 26 (1866) "Prelude" (Ger. *Vorspiel*). It is in sonata form, but its brevity and lack of highly contrasting themes do indeed imbue it with an introductory character.

- **C.** What it introduces is the second movement (*adagio*), the heart and soul of the concerto. Rarely do we hear music better suited to the lyric capabilities of the violin. **Musical selection:** Bruch, Violin Concerto no. 1 in G Minor, op. 26, movement 2, opening.
- **D.** The third movement in sonata form opens with a fabulous gypsy-style dance. **Musical selection:** Bruch, Violin Concerto no. 1 in G Minor, op. 26, movement 3, theme 1.

IV. There was a time in the early 20th century when the single most beloved concerto in the repertoire was that of Edvard Hagerup Grieg. **Musical selection:** Grieg, Piano Concerto in A Minor, op. 16, movement 1, opening.

- **A.** Edvard Grieg (1843–1907) was born in Bergen, Norway, and died there 64 years later. He built his compositional reputation on miniatures for piano and songs for piano and voice. His favorite composer was Frederic Chopin, and he was thrilled when critics referred to him as the "Chopin of the north." He wrote no symphonies and relatively few orchestral works. The Piano Concerto in A Minor of 1868 is the only concerto he completed. He continued to revise it to the end of his life.
- **B.** Unlike his other works, the concerto was not so much influenced by Norwegian folk music as it was by Robert Schumann's Piano Concerto in A Minor.
  - **1.** Grieg studied at the Leipzig Conservatory, which had been founded by Felix Mendelssohn and where Robert Schumann had been a faculty member.
  - **2.** Despite his later claim that he hated the German rigidity of the conservatory, Grieg forged friendships at Leipzig that would shape much of his professional life. These included his piano teacher, Ernst Ferdinand Wensel, who had been a friend of Mendelssohn and Schumann. Through Wensel, Grieg developed a lifelong love for Robert Schumann's music.
- **C.** Like Schumann's piano concerto, Grieg's concerto begins with an explosive orchestral introduction. This is followed by a dramatic chordal descent in the piano, which in turn, is followed by a surprisingly quiet and melancholy theme, played first by the orchestra, then by the piano. In the following musical excerpts, we compare the opening measures of the Schumann and Grieg concerti. **Musical selections:** Schumann, Piano Concerto in A

Minor, op. 54, movement 1, theme 1; Grieg, Piano Concerto in A Minor, op. 16, movement 1, opening.
1. Schumann's influence on Grieg's concerto is pervasive, from the common key of A minor and the partnership between the orchestra and soloist to the formal structures of the individual movements. Grieg diverges from Schumann's model, however, in his use of the piano. Grieg's solo part is much more virtuosic than Schumann's. In its brilliance and technical demands, it is genuinely Lisztian.
2. Grieg told a story of how Liszt, impressed by Grieg's music, invited him to visit Rome, where Liszt proceeded to sight-read Grieg's Sonata for Violin and Piano in G Major, playing both parts at once and not missing a single note. Liszt also sight-read Grieg's piano concerto, solo part and orchestral part simultaneously, providing a running commentary as he played. Impressed, he complimented Grieg and told him he would have a successful career.
3. The second movement of Grieg's concerto is one of the most beautiful *adagios* in the repertoire, a wonderful example of what Tchaikovsky meant when he praised Grieg for "that rarest of qualities: perfect simplicity" (Steinberg, p. 203). In this excerpt, we advance to a point roughly halfway through the movement, where the piano dramatically plays the movement's principal theme. **Musical selection:** Grieg, Piano Concerto in A Minor, op. 16, movement 2.
4. The third-movement finale exhibits the most explicit influence of Norwegian folk music in the concerto. **Musical selection:** Grieg, Piano Concerto in A Minor, op. 16, movement 3, opening. Would that Grieg had composed more than one concerto!

V. Of the many piano concerti written during the second half of the 19th century, all but a few have been forgotten. The survivors include Tchaikovsky's first piano concerto, both of Brahms's piano concerti, Grieg's piano concerto, and Saint-Saens' second piano concerto. Two piano concerti from this period have been unfairly neglected. They are by the Polish composers Moritz Moszkowski (1854–1925) and Ignaz Paderewski (1860–1941), men who were famous for their wit.

A. Moszkowski wrote two concerti, one for violin and one for piano. The piano concerto (1898) is a genuine symphony with piano soloist: It is four movements long, with a third-movement scherzo. It was undoubtedly modeled after Brahms's four-movement second piano concerto of 1881. Moszkowski's is a big, long, elegant, upbeat work, especially notable for its brilliant pianism and its sparkling, memorable themes.

    B. The first movement begins with a ruminative theme in the orchestra; when played by the piano, it becomes lyric and passionate. **Musical selection:** Moszkowski, Piano Concerto in E Major, op. 59, movement 1.

    C. The second movement is a wry and delicate *andante*, sort of like Mahler without the angst. **Musical selection:** Moszkowski, Piano Concerto in E Major, op. 59, movement 2.

    D. The third-movement scherzo is a spectacular tour-de-force for piano. **Musical selection:** Moszkowski, Piano Concerto in E Major, op. 59, movement 3.

    E. In the fourth movement, Moszkowski appropriated a tune from the third movement of Tchaikovsky's second piano concerto of 1880, but he made it his own. **Musical selection:** Moszkowski, Piano Concerto in E Major, op. 59, movement 4, opening. We will compare the Moszkowski version with its inspiration in the next lecture.

VI. Ignaz Paderewski was a late bloomer, whose career as a pianist did not really begin until he was in his early 30s. He composed most of the music for which he is remembered today, including his Piano Concerto in A Minor, before his career as a pianist was established.

    A. Paderewski's only piano concerto, completed in 1888, features the same sort of highly stylized Polish dance rhythms that we hear in the music of his hero, Frederic Chopin. An example of this is found in the rondo in the third and final movement, marked *allegro molto vivace* ("fast, with a lot of life"). It is a Polish dance filled with spectacular virtuosic pyrotechnics. **Musical selection:** Paderewski, Piano Concerto in A Minor, op. 17, movement 3, rondo theme and first contrasting episode, opening.

    B. Paderewski's patriotism went far beyond his music. In 1919, he became prime minister and minister of foreign affairs in a newly independent Poland and was Poland's representative at and signer of the Versailles Treaty. When World War II broke out, he came to the United States, where he died in 1941. In 1992, his body was returned to Poland for a state funeral and buried at St. John's Cathedral in Warsaw. His heart, however, remains in the United States at the shrine of the Black Madonna in Doylestown, Pennsylvania.

VII. Richard Strauss's long career began in the 19th century and ended in the mid-20th century. He composed four concerti: one for violin, two for horn, and one for oboe. In this lecture, we examine the first horn concerto of 1883 and the oboe concerto of 1945.

  A. Strauss (1864–1949) was trained to be a composer and pianist. His father was also principal horn player at the Munich court orchestra for 49 years; thus, the sound of the horn was very familiar to Strauss.

  B. Strauss Sr. had no tolerance for "modern" music, such as that of Wagner, which explains the relatively conservative style of his son's earliest works, including the Horn Concerto no. 1. Although conservative, this is a brilliant work, perfectly suited to the horn. **Musical selection:** Strauss, Horn Concerto no. 1 in Eb Major, op. 11, movement 3, conclusion.

  C. Strauss's Oboe Concerto in D Major was inspired by an American army officer, John de Lancie, whose prewar (and postwar) career was as an oboist. De Lancie met Strauss in Germany at the end of World War II and gave Strauss the idea of writing an oboe concerto.

   1. Strauss's oboe concerto is a masterwork of elegance, melodic grace, and concision, though it begins with a passage that strikes fear in the heart of every oboist: After two brief trills in the 'cellos, the oboe enters and plays for 57 measures non-stop, without a single rest during which to take a breath. To play this passage, the oboist must use a technique called *circular breathing*, during which the oboist must exhale air held in the cheeks while simultaneously inhaling through the nose.

   2. The opening minute of the first movement is an example of Strauss's music at the end of his career, still informed by a Romantic sensibility but stripped down to its barest and most essential elements. **Musical selection:** Concerto for Oboe and Small Orchestra in D Major, movement 1, opening.

Lecture Thirteen
Tchaikovsky

Scope: Tchaikovsky's overly sensitive nature made him vulnerable to criticism, and few major composers have been subject to as much criticism, often damning criticism, as Tchaikovsky. Of all Tchaikovsky's works, his three completed concerti (Piano Concerto no. 1 in Bb Minor, Piano Concerto no. 2 in G Major, and Violin Concerto in D Major) received the most criticism: They were called too long, too difficult—his violin concerto was described as "unplayable"—tasteless, sprawling, and banal. Tchaikovsky took a German approach to concerto composition in his adoption of structural ideas, but he used these structures loosely, with his Russian predilection for thematic variety and dramatic spontaneity. His hybrid compositional style sat neither in the German camp nor the Russian, and this is what incensed both the German pedants and the Russian nationalists. Yet, ultimately, Tchaikovsky's concerti triumphed to become cornerstones of the repertoire. Their virtues outweigh their flaws, and this is especially true of his Piano Concerto no. 1 in Bb Minor and his fabulous Violin Concerto in D Major, his single greatest work and one of the great concerti of the 19th century.

Outline

I. Peter Ilyich Tchaikovsky (1840–1893) was one of the most overly sensitive men and over-criticized major composers in the history of Western music. He was right to be nervous about his compositional technique, which often failed him. For example, at the climactic moment in his *1812* Overture, op 49. Tchaikovsky wrote a transition that is incredibly pedestrian. **Musical selection:** *1812* Overture, op. 49 (1882), transition. Tchaikovsky himself confessed his lack of skill in the "management of form."

    A. None of Tchaikovsky's works was subjected to more scathing criticism than his three completed concerti—two for piano and one for violin. They were disparaged as too long, too difficult (even unplayable, as in the case of the violin concerto), tasteless, sprawling, and banal. Yet all of them triumphed in the end.

B. In 1862, at the age of 22, Tchaikovsky enrolled at the brand new St. Petersburg Conservatory, founded by Anton Rubinstein, an internationally known pianist, composer, and conductor.
  1. Rubinstein was German-trained, and he intended to create a German-styled educational institution in what he considered to be a backward Russian musical environment.
  2. Rubinstein's ideals did not sit well with Russian nationalist composers, who claimed that Russian art music should be based on the models of the Russian language and folk music.
  3. They waged an impassioned debate with Rubinstein and the so-called internationalists, who believed that Russian music could benefit from the time-proven compositional methods and models of Western European music.

C. Tchaikovsky did relatively well at the conservatory, although he never learned to compose a convincing development section. He came to the attention of Anton Rubinstein, who was opening another conservatory in Moscow, where Anton's brother Nicolai was to be director. Rubinstein offered Tchaikovsky a position on the Moscow faculty, which Tchaikovsky accepted.

D. An early work by Tchaikovsky received a ruthless review by the Russian composer and critic Cesar Cui. Tchaikovsky was devastated. It took him years to tame his fear that he would be discovered for the fraud he believed himself to be, and his longing for approval only made things worse.

E. Tchaikovsky composed his first piano concerto in six weeks between November and December of 1874 and completed the orchestration in February of 1875. He assumed that his friend and mentor Nicolai Rubinstein would premiere the concerto as piano soloist, just as he had, and would, premiere many of Tchaikovsky's works in his capacity as a conductor.
  1. In December 1874, Tchaikovsky asked Rubinstein to review the nearly completed concerto. Tchaikovsky played the first movement. **Musical selection:** Tchaikovsky, Piano Concerto no. 1 in Bb Minor, op. 23, movement 1, introduction. Rubinstein offered no comment.
  2. Tchaikovsky played the second movement, the beginning of which is scored for flute and pizzicato strings. **Musical selection:** Tchaikovsky, Piano Concerto no. 1 in Bb Minor,

op. 23, movement 2, opening. Still no response from Rubinstein.

3. Tchaikovsky played the rondo of the third and final movement, which is based on a Ukrainian folk song. **Musical selection:** Tchaikovsky, Piano Concerto no. 1 in Bb Minor, op. 23, movement 3, conclusion.

4. When Tchaikovsky finished playing, Rubinstein remained silent until pressed for a comment by Tchaikovsky. Then, he expressed his opinion in no uncertain terms, calling the work "worthless…unplayable…vulgar," among other things. He recommended that Tchaikovsky throw most of it away. Tchaikovsky insisted that he would publish his concerto exactly the way it was.

5. What Rubinstein was criticizing were the structural liberties and seemingly arbitrary musical events that offended his German-trained musical soul. For example, the first movement begins with a theme that is the single most recognizable passage in the concerto: a Slavic theme played by the strings, accompanied by huge, thrumming chords in the piano, followed by a magnificent piano cadenza and a further impassioned playing of the opening theme in the strings. **Musical selection:** Tchaikovsky, Piano Concerto no. 1 in Bb Minor, op. 23, movement 1, opening.

6. Rubinstein's problem with this opening theme is that it is never heard again. Tchaikovsky tacked it on to the beginning of the concerto because he liked the way it sounded. Rubinstein expected Tchaikovsky to compose as a German composer did: linearly, logically, and sensibly, rather than in the style of a Russian composer, for whom thematic variety and moment-to-moment drama are much more important than preexisting forms and rhetorical development.

F. Tchaikovsky's music often sounds German but acts Russian, while at other times, it sounds Russian but acts German.

G. The concerto's virtues far outweigh its flaws—if they are flaws—as history has borne out. But in 1875, Tchaikovsky was battling with the problem of finding a pianist willing to learn and premiere the work. Eventually, the virtuoso pianist Hans von Bülow agreed to premiere the work, and he even fell in love with it.

H. Tchaikovsky dedicated the concerto to von Bülow, who premiered it in Boston on October 25, 1875. The concerto was ecstatically received by the Bostonians. Von Bülow performed the concerto 139 times during his American tour, establishing the concerto and the name of Tchaikovsky across the United States.

I. Eventually, the "flaws" of the concerto came to be perceived as special aspects that made the work unique. By 1878, it had become an audience favorite throughout Europe and the Americas. That same year, Nicolai Rubinstein apologized to Tchaikovsky, learned the "unplayable" piano part, and went on to become one of the concerto's greatest champions.

II. Thrilled with Nicolai Rubinstein's change of heart, he wrote Rubinstein another piano concerto. As he had done initially with the first concerto, he dedicated the second concerto (1880) to Rubinstein and sent him the score. Rubinstein's reaction was positive at first, but a few months later, Rubinstein began to criticize the work.

A. The premiere was delayed, and in the end, Rubinstein did not premiere the concerto because he died in 1881. The task fell to Rubinstein's protégé, Sergei Ivanovich Taneyev, who had been a composition student of Tchaikovsky at the Moscow Conservatory. Taneyev also criticized the work.

1. Taneyev found the first and second movements too long. In this, he was right, and Tchaikovsky knew it. He made some cuts, but the inordinate length of the concerto bothered him to the day he died.

2. Four years after Tchaikovsky's death, a drastically edited version of the concerto was published. This version, by Alexander Ilyich Siloti, is a butchery.

B. In the following excerpt, we hear the opening of the third movement, which is in a sort of sonata form/rondo form. **Musical selection:** Tchaikovsky, Piano Concerto no. 2 in G Major, op. 44, movement 3, opening.

C. As mentioned earlier, Moszkowski borrowed this theme for his Piano Concerto in E Major. **Musical selection**: Moszkowski, Piano Concerto in E Major, op. 59, movement 4, theme.

D. Tchaikovsky began a third piano concerto in 1888 but completed only the first movement, which was published independently as op. 75. After Tchaikovsky's death, Taneyev attempted to complete the second and third movements from Tchaikovsky's sketches. This reconstructed concerto is almost never performed, although Tchaikovsky's first movement is excellent.

III. In my opinion, Tchaikovsky's Violin Concerto in D Major is his single greatest work and one of the handful of the greatest concerti of the 19th century.

    A. As was so often the case with Tchaikovsky, the actual composition of the work went smoothly. It was the drama surrounding its first performance that drove Tchaikovsky crazy.

    B. Tchaikovsky wrote his violin concerto while staying at Clarens on Lake Geneva in Switzerland. He was recovering from a disastrous marriage and an attempted suicide. One of his visitors at Clarens was the violinist Yosif Kotek, Tchaikovsky's bisexual former lover. Feeling reborn and inspired, Tchaikovsky sketched and orchestrated his entire violin concerto in under a month.

    C. Tchaikovsky wanted to dedicate the work to Kotek but was afraid of the gossip he believed the dedication would inspire. Instead, he dedicated the concerto to his Moscow Conservatory colleague, the violinist Leopold Auer. Tchaikovsky knew Auer's fame and popularity would give the concerto the sort of caché that would ensure its success.

    D. When Auer pronounced the solo part "impossible to play," Tchaikovsky went back to Kotek and again offered him the dedication and premiere performance. However, Kotek, peeved that Tchaikovsky had approached Auer, refused the offer and declared the piece unplayable, even though he had played it through while it was being composed.

    E. For the next two and a half years, Tchaikovsky kept revising the solo part until, finally, the Russian violinist Adolf Brodsky consented to perform the premiere, which took place in Vienna on December 4, 1881, at a Vienna Philharmonic Society concert. The performance went well, but the reviews were savage. The Viennese critic Eduard Hanslick literally used the word "stink" to describe Tchaikovsky's music. Tchaikovsky was so offended by this review that he memorized it and could recite it in the original German to the day he died. It is difficult to fathom how such a beautiful concerto could have elicited such a review.

F. The first movement is in sonata form with an introduction, which begins with a quiet and elegant tune presented by the orchestral violins. Taking a page from his Piano Concerto no. 1, Tchaikovsky's introductory melody will not be heard again; its raison d'être is to set the lyric table for the solo violin. **Musical selection:** Tchaikovsky, Violin Concerto in D Major, op. 35, movement 1, introduction.

    1. The violin enters with a beautiful little cadenza. **Musical selection:** Tchaikovsky, Violin Concerto in D Major, op. 35, movement 1, violin entry.

    2. The solo violin now plays theme 1, a theme of otherworldly beauty. This is Tchaikovsky's lyric art at its highest level. The violin becomes a genuinely operatic voice. **Musical selection:** Tchaikovsky, Violin Concerto in D Major, op. 35, movement 1, theme 1.

    3. The modulating bridge follows. It builds to a climax before quieting in preparation for theme 2, which will also be introduced by the solo violin. Marked *con molto expressivo* ("with great expression"), theme 2 is yet another lyric triumph, structured in three long, exquisite phrases. There is a hint of minor, a hint of darkness, giving it a touch of Slavic angst. Tchaikovsky's orchestral accompaniment is spare and extremely effective, while the theme, when played on the violin's G string during its third and final phrase, has an almost chocolate richness to it. **Musical selection:** Tchaikovsky, Violin Concerto in D Major, op. 35, movement 1, theme 2.

G. The development section features a series of thematic restatements and variations, rather than traditional thematic development. It is based almost entirely on theme 1 and begins with a majestic and martial version of the theme, played by the orchestra. Finally, after playing almost continuously for more than six minutes, the solo violin gets a rest. **Musical selection:** Tchaikovsky, Violin Concerto in D Major, op. 35, movement 1, development section, part 1.

    1. The violin soon re-enters, playing a delicate but exceedingly virtuosic version of theme 1. **Musical selection:** Tchaikovsky, Violin Concerto in D Major, op. 35, movement 1, development section, part 3.

      2. The rest of the development features restatements and variations of theme 1, separated by brief transitional episodes. It concludes with the cadenza, a strategy we first observed in the first movement of Mendelssohn's violin concerto. The violin trill that concludes the cadenza continues into the recapitulation, effectively bridging the two sections. A solo flute plays the first phrase of theme 1 in the recapitulation. **Musical selection:** Tchaikovsky, Violin Concerto in D Major, op. 35, movement 1, development section, conclusion, and recapitulation, opening.

      3. In the coda, contrary to the rules of sonata form, neither theme 1 nor theme 2 will be heard from. Instead, an exceedingly virtuosic solo violin leads the movement to a blistering and jubilant conclusion. **Musical selection:** Tchaikovsky, Violin Concerto in D Major, op. 35, movement 1, coda.

H. The two remaining movements of the concerto are just as fabulous as the first. The final minute of the third movement might well be the most viscerally exciting music ever composed.

I. Tchaikovsky's Violin Concerto in D Major quickly became a pillar of the repertoire, which it remains to this day. Leopold Auer, like Nicolai Rubinstein before him, realized he had made a big mistake and apologized to Tchaikovsky. He learned the violin part and became one of the concerto's greatest champions, performing it everywhere and introducing it to his students, among them Mischa Elman and Jascha Heifetz.

Lecture Fourteen
Brahms and the Symphonic Concerto

Scope: Brahms's compositional style is a wonderful synthesis of the clear and concise musical forms and genres of the Classical and Baroque eras and the melodic, harmonic, and expressive palette of the Romantic era in which he lived. What he rejected in the Romantic philosophy was its conception of music as a partner with other arts, particularly literature, resulting in the composite art form known as *program music*. He was also averse to the Romantic idea of the virtuoso as hero. Although his piano music is certainly virtuosic, it does not celebrate virtuosity for its own sake; in his Piano Concerto no. 2 in Bb Major, the piano is treated like a second orchestra. As just one example of this, there is no true piano cadenza in this work. Indeed, Brahms's approach to the concerto is notably symphonic—a tour-de-force of motivic development. We follow our in-depth examination of Brahms's monumental second piano concerto with a brief look at his last orchestral work, the Double Concerto for Violin and 'Cello in A Minor, op. 102.

Outline

I. Johannes Brahms (1833–1897) wrote four concerti: two piano concerti, a violin concerto, and a double concerto for violin and 'cello. (For an in-depth examination of the violin concerto, see Professor Greenberg's Teaching Company course *Concert Masterworks*. For a discussion of the Piano Concerto no. 1 in D Minor, see Lectures Three and Four of the Teaching Company course *Great Masters: Brahms—His Life and Music*.) This lecture will deal primarily with Brahms's Piano Concerto no. 2 in Bb Major of 1881. As a postscript, we will take a brief look at Brahms's wonderful Double Concerto for Violin and 'Cello in A Minor, op. 102 of 1887, his last orchestral work.

    A. By 1863, when he was 30 years old, Brahms's mature compositional priorities and aesthetic were firmly in place. They represented a wonderful if paradoxical combination of head and heart: a synthesis of Classical discipline and Romantic expression.

1. Brahms believed in the clarity and concision of the musical forms of the Classical and Baroque eras. But he was also a man of his time, and he used all the melodic and harmonic resources of the Romantic era to express what he wanted to express.
2. To this very day, Brahms is sometimes called a "Classicist" because of his predilection for using the genres and forms of the Classical era. However, there is nothing Classical about the melodic, harmonic, or expressive content of Brahms's music. Its musical content and emotional impact are entirely Romantic.
3. What Brahms did not believe in were the theories and musico-political dogma of the New German School, with its claim that the future of music lay in its fusion with other arts, particularly literature, creating a composite art form called *program music*.

B. Brahms was a superb pianist and could have made a career as a hero-style Romantic virtuoso, had he not been a composer of genius who entirely rejected the whole "virtuoso-as-hero," "artist-as-God" philosophy. Paradoxically, his Piano Concerto no. 2 in Bb Major is a virtuoso work that Brahms himself called "the long terror."
   1. The solo piano part of this concerto is monumentally difficult and requires great intelligence to play. Yet it merges seamlessly with the orchestra and reflects little glory back on the soloist.
   2. The key to this work is that the virtuosity of the solo part arises *not* from Brahms's desire to celebrate the soloist but, rather, from his conception of the solo piano as, in effect, a second orchestra.
   3. Everything about this concerto is symphonic, from its treatment of the piano to its four-movement scheme. Characteristically, the work is a tour-de-force of motivic development, by which he builds almost everything we hear from the simplest melodic means.

C. Our objectives in examining this concerto will be:
   1. To see how Brahms treats the piano like a second orchestra.
   2. To observe Brahms's stunning developmental craft.

II. Theme 1 of the first movement consists of three elements: a quiet opening version of the theme, followed by a dramatic piano interlude, followed by a majestic version of the theme. **Musical selection:** Brahms, Piano Concerto no. 2 in Bb Major, op. 83, movement 1, exposition 1, theme 1.

- **A.** The theme and the movement begin almost as in a dream, with a dialogue between two "orchestras"—between a solo horn and the solo piano. **Musical selection:** Brahms, Piano Concerto no. 2 in Bb Major, op. 83, movement 1, exposition 1, theme 1, phrase 1.
  1. This opening phrase is answered and extended by a gently descending passage heard first in the winds, then in the winds and strings. **Musical selection:** Brahms, Piano Concerto no. 2 in Bb Major, op. 83, movement 1, exposition 1, theme 1, phrase 2.
  2. The opening phrase—the dialogue between the horn and the piano—is built almost entirely from a series of stepwise, three-note melodic ideas, or *motives*. **Piano example #1.**
  3. This motive will become the generative element of the entire movement. Brahms will use it in two ways: He will transform it into a stunning variety of related musical ideas, and he will use it verbatim, as a musical signpost that signals both the beginnings and endings of the large sections of this movement. It is in its second capacity—as a signpost—that we will call this motive a *motto*.
  4. The second phrase of the opening portion of the theme is extended by a gently descending passage heard first in the winds, then in the winds and strings. **Piano examples #2a and #2b.**
  5. Brahms then darkens the harmonic skies by adding just a hint of minor, preparing the way for the dramatic piano interlude. **Piano example #3.**
  6. A majestic version of the theme follows the piano interlude, full of rising and falling three-note mottos. **Musical selection:** Brahms, Piano Concerto no. 2 in Bb Major, op. 83, movement 1, exposition 1, theme 1, majestic version.
- **B.** Brahms uses theme 1 and its motto to articulate the sonata-form structure of the movement.
  1. The second exposition, which is neither a repeat of the first nor a solo exposition, begins with an extended version of

theme 1, in which the motto becomes increasingly important, not just as part of the theme but as a self-standing unit unto itself. **Musical selection:** Brahms, Piano Concerto no. 2 in Bb Major, op. 83, movement 1, exposition 2, theme 1.

2. The development section begins with a calm but mysterious version of theme 1, shared between—again—the horn and the piano, accompanied by tremolo (shivering) strings. **Musical selection:** Brahms, Piano Concerto no. 2 in Bb Major, op. 83, movement 1, development section, opening.

3. The recapitulation begins with an exquisite, dreamscape-like version of theme 1, heard in dialogue between—again—the horn and the piano. **Musical selection:** Brahms, Piano Concerto no. 2 in Bb Major, op. 83, movement 1, recapitulation, theme 1.

4. Last, the coda begins, with theme 1 heard initially in the horn over a deep trill on the piano. **Musical selection:** Brahms, Piano Concerto no. 2 in Bb Major, op. 83, movement 1, coda, opening.

5. Just as theme 1 initiates the large sections of the movement, so the motto concludes the large sections of the movement. The coda ends in a deluge of descending mottos. **Musical selection:** Brahms, Piano Concerto no. 2 in Bb Major, op. 83, movement 1, coda, conclusion.

6. Going back to the beginning of the movement, we see that Brahms concludes the first exposition with a long string of mottos heard as units unto themselves, disengaged from theme 1. This motto-dominated "cadence material" concludes with a huge, six-octave-wide motto in the solo piano, followed by an ascending/descending passage in octaves leading directly to theme 1 in the second exposition. **Musical selection:** Brahms, Piano Concerto no. 2 in Bb Major, op. 83, movement 1, exposition 1, cadence material.

7. In both expositions and the recapitulation, theme 2 is introduced by a string of five mottos, moving downward in the orchestra. **Musical selection:** Brahms, Piano Concerto no. 2 in Bb Major, op. 83, movement 1, exposition 2, modulating bridge.

8. The final part of the development section begins with three *fortissimo* mottos in the orchestra that together initiate the

transition to the recapitulation. **Musical selection:** Brahms, Piano Concerto no. 2 in Bb Major, op. 83, movement 1, retransition.
- C. Theme 2 is a rich, sinuous, very Brahmsian theme that shifts constantly between F major and D minor. It ends with the motto. **Musical selection:** Brahms, Piano Concerto no. 2 in Bb Major, op. 83, movement 1, theme 2.
    1. There is nothing like good motivic development to create a sense of unity among the seemingly diverse elements of a piece of music. For example, theme 1 began this way: **Piano example #5a.**
    2. Then Brahms flipped that upside down: **Piano example #5b.**
    3. Brahms then took this "upside down" phrase and extended it to create the next phrase of theme 1. **Back-to-back piano examples, #5b and #5c.**
    4. Brahms embellished this descending phrase and, in doing so, created theme 2. **Back-to-back piano examples, #5c and #5d.**
- D. The piano plays a dramatic version of theme 2 in the second exposition. **Musical selection:** Brahms, Piano Concerto no. 2 in Bb Major, op. 83, movement 1, exposition 2, theme 2.
- E. The solo piano part, for all its terrifying virtuosity, is inseparable from the orchestra in terms of the ongoing musical development of the movement. Nowhere is the integrated nature of the piano part clearer than in the dramatic piano interlude that is heard during the course of theme 1. **Musical selection:** Brahms, Piano Concerto no. 2 in Bb Major, op. 83, movement 1, exposition 1, dramatic piano interlude.
    1. This interlude allows the piano to establish its bona fides as a soloist early in the movement, but more than that, it paves the way for theme 2 and even anticipates certain essential elements of theme 2.
    2. The dramatic piano interlude is in four parts. In the first part, roiling, dissonant arpeggios in the bass accompany a series of progressively higher falling semitones. **Piano example #6.**
    3. These falling semitones grow directly out of the second phrase of theme 1. **Piano example #7.**

    4. By isolating the falling semitones from the second phrase of theme 1, Brahms is also anticipating the first three notes of theme 2, which just happens to begin with a falling semitone. **Piano example #8a** (dramatic piano interlude, part 1); **piano example #8b** (theme 2, opening).

  F. When we finally hear theme 2, it concludes with a phrase based on this very same descending semitone passage. **Musical selection:** Brahms, Piano Concerto no. 2 in Bb Major, op. 83, movement 1, exposition 1, theme 2, orchestral conclusion.

  G. Let us hear the first exposition in its entirety: theme 1, heard initially in a quiet dialogue between the horn and the piano; the dramatic piano interlude; the heroic conclusion of theme 1 and a series of mottos; theme 2, concluding with a motto; the descending-semitone-inspired passage; and finally, a series of mottos, first in the orchestra, then in the solo piano, bringing the first exposition to its conclusion. **Musical selection:** Brahms, Piano Concerto no. 2 in Bb Major, op. 83, movement 1, exposition 1.

  H. This music displays a high information content, and we have hardly scratched the surface. The key point here is that for all the virtuosity of the music, the piano is not treated like a heroic soloist but like a second orchestra, because the intent of the music is more symphonic than soloistic.

III. The second-movement scherzo makes the symphonic scope of this concerto crystal clear. This is the sort of middle movement we would expect to hear in a four-movement symphony but certainly not in a three-movement concerto.

  A. Again, the piano is treated as an orchestra unto itself; again, the level of motivic development and metamorphosis in this movement is stunning; again, a Classical clarity of form showcases music of thrilling Romantic expressive content.

  B. A scherzo is an up-tempo, three-part form, schematicized as A–B–A (idea–departure–return).

    1. Brahms's opening A section is dominated by thematic material based on a trill (the back-and-forth alternation of two adjacent pitches). The movement begins with a dramatic, trill-like motive, followed by an upward leap. **Piano example #9a.**

2. After this, in a tranquil and mysterious passage, we hear another trill-based melody. **Piano example #9b. Musical selection:** Brahms, Piano Concerto no. 2 in Bb Major, op. 83, movement 2, opening.
3. In performance, this entire passage will be repeated, after which a further development of these ideas will be heard, all of it encompassing the opening A section of the movement.
4. The contrasting middle B section of the movement is in D major. As compact and sinuous as is the thematic material for the A section, so open and triadic is the thematic material for section B. **Piano example #10a.**
5. Accompanying the B theme is an inverted version of the trill melody heard during the tranquil portion of the A section. **Piano example #10b.**
6. How Brahms transits from the opening A section in D minor to the contrasting B section in D major remains one of the great moments in Western art: The trilling motive of part A is repeated over and over again. Suddenly, the trilling gives way to the middle section of the movement in D major, with its widely spaced melody and rhythmically leisurely pace. The effect is incredible—like the relief of emerging from an extremely restrictive confinement to wide-open spaces. **Musical selection:** Brahms, Piano Concerto no. 2 in Bb Major, op. 83, movement 2, scherzo–trio, A, conclusion, and B, opening.

IV. The third movement (*andante*) finally offers the piano a break. The movement opens with a gorgeous, lightly scored passage, in which a solo 'cello takes the lead. **Musical selection:** Brahms, Piano Concerto no. 2 in Bb Major, op. 83, movement 3, opening.

V. The fourth movement is a sonata rondo—a rondo that features among its contrasting episodes a development section based on the rondo theme. Labeled *allegretto grazioso*, it is one of the most graceful and engaging movements that Brahms ever composed.
  A. The movement has three main thematic elements: the rondo theme (theme A) and contrasting themes B and C. The rondo theme itself has the grace and flavor of a Hungarian dance. **Musical selection:** Brahms, Piano Concerto no. 2 in Bb Major, op. 83, movement 4, rondo theme, opening.

1. The first contrasting episode features two distinct themes, which we will call B and C. The opening of theme B is filled with a sort of calculated mock *schmerz*, though it quickly takes on a lighter tone. **Musical selection:** Brahms, Piano Concerto no. 2 in Bb Major, op. 83, movement 4, theme B.
2. Theme C is filled with pop and fizz. **Musical selection:** Brahms, Piano Concerto no. 2 in Bb Major, op. 83, movement 4, theme C.

B. Most telling in this wonderful concerto is the fact that, except for the dramatic piano interlude in the first movement, there is virtually nothing we can identify as a cadenza in any of the four movements. The passages that the piano plays by itself were not intended, nor are they perceived, as cadenzas. Everything serves the greater musical good, not the soloist.

VI. Brahms's Double Concerto for Violin and 'Cello in A Minor, op. 102, of 1887 was his last orchestral work and composed as a peace offering to his friend, the violinist Joseph Joachim.

A. Brahms, an ornery personality, was not disposed toward peace offerings, but in 1884, he made a mistake, and he knew it.
1. Joachim, a jealous man, believed that his wife, Amalie, was having an affair with a music publisher. Brahms, who was convinced of Amalie's innocence, wrote her a letter of support. Amalie produced his letter in court, and it greatly helped to convince the judge of her innocence. Joachim was enraged at what he considered to be Brahms's treachery, and he severed their relationship.
2. Uncharacteristically, Brahms regretted what he had done and wrote the Double Concerto for Violin and 'Cello, with solo parts composed specifically for Joachim and the 'cellist in Joachim's string quartet, Robert Hausmann, as a peace offering. Joachim consented to perform the work, and Brahms dedicated it to him.

B. The Double Concerto is a gorgeous, lyric, three-movement work and the first important concerto for more than one instrument to appear in the second half of the 19th century. It is a perfect embodiment of Brahms's compositional priorities, based, as it is, on the principles of the Classical-era sinfonia concertante, but informed by the melodic, harmonic, and expressive substance of the Romantic era.

Lecture Fifteen
Dvorak

Scope: Antonin Dvorak's career as a composer was helped in no small way by Johannes Brahms, who was impressed by the young Bohemian's music and recommended him to the publisher Fritz Simrock. Brahms and Dvorak, who became close friends, held the same musical beliefs, which included an appreciation for Mozart and the spare, clear constructs of Classical-era music, infused with a Beethovenian expressivity and a Romantic melodic and harmonic language. Famous for his "nationalist" approach to music, Dvorak attracted the attention of the founders of the National Conservatory of Music in New York, who offered him the position of director of the conservatory. Dvorak accepted and spent the years 1892–1895 in the United States. His compositional output during those years included the Symphony in E Minor (*New World*), the String Quartets nos. 12 and 13, and the 'Cello Concerto in B Minor. The latter work—one of three concerti by Dvorak—is not only the finest work he wrote but also the greatest 'cello concerto in the repertoire. Its first movement represents a deeply moving journey from darkness to light. It is followed by one of the great slow movements in the concerto repertoire. Its poignancy, inspired by the death of a loved one, is heartbreaking. The dramatic third-movement finale comes to a dazzling and triumphant culmination, capped with a coda that miraculously captures the essence of a range of powerful emotions.

Outline

I. Antonin Dvorak's 'Cello Concerto in B Minor, is, along with the violin concerti of Brahms and Tchaikovsky, the greatest string concerto composed during the second half of the 19th century and, by general consensus, the greatest single concerto ever composed for the 'cello.

   A. The music of Antonin Dvorak (1841–1904) inspired an enthusiastic Johannes Brahms to bring Dvorak to the attention of his own publisher, Fritz Simrock, recommending that Simrock publish Dvorak's *Moravian* Duets. Simrock did so, and the duets were so popular that they launched Dvorak's career. Brahms and

Dvorak developed a close friendship that lasted for the rest of their lives.

B. Brahms and Dvorak shared the same musical outlook: They both believed in Mozart and the precision and concision of Classical music, combined with the expressive essence of Beethoven and the melodic and harmonic language of Romanticism.

C. Dvorak, like Brahms, was that rarest of musical creatures: a composer who became rich and famous in his own lifetime. Dvorak's music was popular: Its lilting, un-self-conscious, Czech-flavored melodic surface was—and still is—considered attractive in a way that the more "serious" music of Brahms generally is not.

D. In 1891, Dvorak's fame as a nationalist prompted Jeanette Thurber, one of the founders of the National Conservatory of Music in New York, to offer Dvorak a position. She wanted Dvorak to become the conservatory's director and start an American school of composition. Dvorak accepted the challenge. He remained in the position from 1892–1895. Although he was never particularly at home in the United States, he managed to compose some of his finest music during his stay, including the Symphony in E Minor (*New World*), the String Quartets nos. 12 (*American*) and 13, and the 'Cello Concerto in B Minor.

E. Dvorak wrote three concerti, one each for piano and violin and one for 'cello. The piano concerto is an early work and not representative of Dvorak's best. The Violin Concerto in A Minor, op. 53, is wonderful and worthy of study, but this lecture will be entirely devoted to the 'cello concerto, the greatest 'cello concerto in the repertoire and Dvorak's best composition.

II. The 'cello concerto was composed in New York between November 8, 1894, and February 9, 1895. It was the last work Dvorak completed during his American residence, although he changed the end of the work after he returned to Bohemia.

A. The Czech 'cellist Hanus Wihan had suggested for some time that Dvorak write a 'cello concerto. Dvorak, however, did not think the 'cello suited to solo music. He is believed to have changed his mind when he heard Victor Herbert, principal 'cellist of the Metropolitan Opera, play his own second 'cello concerto in the spring of 1894.

B. The first movement of Dvorak's concerto is in double-exposition form, a construct that we have not encountered since the early 19th century.

C. There is an expressive reason why Dvorak deploys double-exposition form here, and it has to do with the spiritual contrast between light and dark. It is manifest in theme 1: The orchestra introduces the theme in the dark key of B minor, which can be taken as a metaphor for fate. The 'cello, which will not go gently into the dark night of B minor, can be seen as the voice of the individual, striving against fate; ultimately, it will attain a state of grace, as represented by the key of B major. The first movement is a metaphor for a long, deeply moving journey from darkness to triumphant brilliance.

D. Theme 1 in the orchestral exposition is in three phrases: The first, quiet and characterized by march-like rhythms and played by clarinets, bassoons, and low strings, has a dirge-like quality. **Musical selection:** Dvorak, 'Cello Concerto in B Minor, op. 104, movement 1, orchestral exposition, theme 1, phrase 1.

    1. The second phrase of the theme also begins quietly but quickly builds to a climax. **Musical selection:** Dvorak, 'Cello Concerto in B Minor, op. 104, movement 1, orchestral exposition, theme 1, phrase 2.

    2. The climactic third phrase, marked *grandioso* ("grandly"), virtually explodes from the orchestra. This is magnificent and powerful music, with the march-like quality of the theme now extremely pronounced. The theme concludes with a shimmering, trill-dominated descent that dissipates the accumulated energy. **Musical selections:** Dvorak, 'Cello Concerto in B Minor, op. 104, movement 1, orchestral exposition, theme 1, phrase 3; theme 1 in its entirety.

    3. The solo exposition begins with the 'cello declaiming the opening of theme 1 in B major before shifting back to minor. **Musical selection:** Dvorak, 'Cello Concerto in B Minor, op. 104, movement 1, solo exposition, theme 1. This version of theme 1 is distinctly Slavic in tone and powerfully evocative of the "voice of the individual" attempting to fight the darkness that has characterized theme 1 to this point in the movement.

4. The development section is the dramatic epicenter of the movement. In this movement, the 'cello must deal with the darkness of theme 1 as first expressed in the orchestral exposition and, having done so, overcome that darkness.
5. The climax, at the very center of the development section, is one of the most remarkable passages in the repertoire. It is marked *molto sostenuto* ("very sustained"), and in it, the 'cello plays a somber, almost grieving, profoundly contemplative version of theme 1, accompanied by hushed string tremolos and a gorgeous countermelody in solo flute, hovering above the song of mortality and mortal pain that is being played by the 'cello. **Musical selection:** Dvorak, 'Cello Concerto in B Minor, op. 104, movement 1, development.
6. It is a stunning passage. The 'cello's wonder and awe, grief and pain become ours as well. Having given voice to this complex web of emotions, the mood of the movement now shifts toward the bright side.
7. When we next hear theme 1 right at the end of the recapitulation, the darkness will have been dispelled entirely. Dvorak marks this final passage *grandioso*—it is the most magnificent and extended version of theme 1 in the entire movement, followed by a blaring and joyful coda, an expressive polar opposite to the somber version of theme 1 that began the movement. **Musical selection:** Dvorak, 'Cello Concerto in B Minor, op. 104, movement 1, recapitulation, theme 1 and coda.

E. The virtuosity of the 'cello writing is entirely in the service of the music. There is not a single extraneous passage in this entire concerto, put there simply to glorify the soloist.

F. In addition to the "lead" story of fate and mortality and noble aspirations, there is another story—the love interest, if you will—the exquisitely beautiful theme 2.
1. It first emerges, almost magically, on a solo horn, then a clarinet, then an oboe, and finally, in the violins. **Musical selection:** Dvorak, 'Cello Concerto in B Minor, op. 104, movement 1, orchestral exposition, theme 2.
2. In the solo exposition, the 'cello plays a rich and sonorous version of theme 2, followed by a brief developmental episode of the theme, in which rapid, staccato sextuplets (groups of six

notes) played by the 'cello are overlain by an undulating melody in the winds, derived from the opening of theme 2. **Musical selection:** Dvorak, 'Cello Concerto in B Minor, op. 104, movement 1, solo exposition, theme 2 and developmental episode.

G. In an interesting formal twist, Dvorak begins the recapitulation—and the arrival at the key of B major—with theme 2, rather than theme 1. He does this for two reasons.

  1. First, the development section is entirely about theme 1, and Dvorak rightly decided that a little thematic variety at this point was necessary.

  2. But more importantly, as we have already seen, Dvorak wanted to end the movement with a magnificent and triumphant version of theme 1, which allows him to bookend the movement with two entirely different versions of theme 1: one tragic and the other triumphant.

  3. Having decided to bookend the movement in this way, it was obvious that the best formal solution was to reverse the order of the themes in the recapitulation. **Musical selection:** Dvorak, 'Cello Concerto in B Minor, op. 104, movement 1, recapitulation, theme 2.

  4. We should be aware of one last feature of this movement: The cadence material in both the solo exposition and the recapitulation has a genuinely operatic quality to it, as forceful, recitative-like lines in the 'cello are accompanied by orchestral fanfares and interjections. **Musical selection:** Dvorak, 'Cello Concerto in B Minor, op. 104, movement 1, solo exposition, cadence material.

H. The second movement is marked *adagio ma non troppo* ("slowly but not too slowly"). The structure of the movement is A–B–B–A^1, with the outer A sections being gentle and pastoral in mood and the central B sections being dramatic and passionate in mood.

  1. The first half of the opening A section consists of a glowing, magically beautiful theme in G major, scored with chamber-music-like delicacy. **Musical selection:** Dvorak, 'Cello Concerto in B Minor, op. 104, movement 2, section A, opening.

2. Both B sections begin with an explosive passage in G minor. **Musical selection:** Dvorak, 'Cello Concerto in B Minor, op. 104, movement 2, section B, introduction.
3. What could have inspired such bone-jarring, turmoil-ridden passages? While Dvorak was at work on the concerto, he heard that his sister-in-law, Josefina Kaunitzova, was seriously ill. Thirty years before, Dvorak had been her piano teacher and had fallen in love with her. His feelings were not reciprocated, and Dvorak transferred his affections to Josefina's younger sister Anna, whom he married and with whom he raised a family of eight children. But Dvorak never "got over" Josefina, and when he heard she was ill, he planted the theme of one of his own songs into this second movement.
4. The song, entitled "Leave Me Alone," was a special favorite of Josefina. **Piano example #1:** melody of "Leave Me Alone."
5. In the concerto, the melody sounds like this. **Piano example #2.**
6. In the opening B section of the second movement, the tune is played high in the 'cello's range with searing intensity. **Musical selection:** Dvorak, 'Cello Concerto in B Minor, op. 104, movement 2, section B.
7. This is one of the great slow movements in the concerto repertoire, filled with moments of expressive power far above and beyond your typically lyric but often expressively "lite" middle movement.
8. At one point in the final A section, the solo 'cello is joined by a solo flute, as it was during the climactic moment in the development section of the first movement. The duet between these two instruments is especially poignant. The quiet conclusion of this second movement will break your heart and sets up, perfectly, the opening of the third-movement finale.

I. Like the first movement, the third movement begins starkly and darkly in B minor, and like the first movement, it will end brilliantly and magnificently in B major.
   1. Let's hear the opening of the movement: an introduction and rondo theme in the character of a march, replete with one of the oldest musical devices in the book—a triangle meant to portray the jangling of swords and stirrups. **Musical**

selection: Dvorak, 'Cello Concerto in B Minor, op. 104, movement 3, rondo theme.

2. Once again, the battle against darkness is joined. It is a battle that will be fought by the contrasting themes of this rondo. Theme B—the first contrasting theme—is a tender melody in D major, heard in the 'cello and accompanied by a singing countermelody in the clarinet. **Musical selection:** Dvorak, 'Cello Concerto in B Minor, op. 104, movement 3, theme B.

3. The second contrasting theme—theme C—is a rich, Slavic-tinted theme of great dramatic breadth, heard initially, like theme B, in the key of D major. **Musical selection:** Dvorak, 'Cello Concerto in B Minor, op. 104, movement 3, theme C.

4. The cumulative effect of these gloriously lyric, major-mode contrasting themes is decisive. When the rondo theme returns for the third and final time, it is transformed: What was once dark and dramatic in B minor is now dazzling and triumphant in B major. **Musical selection:** Dvorak, 'Cello Concerto in B Minor, op. 104, movement 3, rondo theme A^2.

5. The coda has a story: On May 27, 1895, Dvorak's sister-in-law died. Dvorak was heartbroken. He removed the last 4 measures from the third and final movement of the concerto and added 67 new measures that display three essential elements:
    a. The first element comprises two quiet notes from theme 1 of the first movement. **Piano example #3.**
    b. The second element is an achingly beautiful passage built from Josefina's favorite song, "Leave Me Alone." **Piano example #4.**
    c. The third element is a blistering and life-affirming final cadence in B major that leaves us in no doubt that the concerto is over. **Piano example #5.**

6. This is music of the most profound peace and resignation; of deep love and affection; of nostalgia for lost youth; of grief, rage, and defiance, all rolled into one miraculous coda. **Musical selection:** Dvorak, 'Cello Concerto in B Minor, op. 104, movement 3, conclusion.

J. Dvorak dedicated the concerto to his friend, the 'cellist Hanus Wihan. When they played it through together, Wihan informed Dvorak that he was not satisfied with the end of the concerto and had taken the liberty of composing a 59-measure cadenza for the third movement, which he had sent to Dvorak's publisher to be published with the score. This cadenza would, obviously, have ruined Dvorak's tribute to his sister-in-law. Dvorak told his publisher not to allow the concerto to be altered by anyone. It is a testament to Dvorak's good nature that he remained friends with Wihan and allowed him to premiere the concerto.

Lecture Sixteen
Rachmaninoff

Scope: Rachmaninoff was one of the great Romantic composers, although he lived well into the 20th century. He possessed transcendental pianistic skills and a phenomenal musical memory. He is best known for his piano music, particularly his piano concerti, the first of which he composed at the age of 19. The piano for Rachmaninoff was, as it had been for Chopin, his musical alter ego. His piano concerti exemplify his compositional style, which was influenced by the music of Tchaikovsky and displays a high degree of lyricism and drama and a preference for the minor mode that often tinges his music with melancholy. His Piano Concerto no. 1 in F# Minor, op. 1, was written in 1891 and revised in 1917. It is a work of stunning precocity but is nowadays overshadowed by his second and third piano concerti. In Piano Concerto no. 2 in C Minor, op. 18, of 1901, we see how Rachmaninoff treats themes as the core of the piece rather than as development resources. He also takes a flexible approach to formal structure. In his Piano Concerto no. 3 in D Minor, op. 30, of 1909, he crafts virtuosic developments from simple beginnings, with one of the most remarkable development sections in the repertoire.

Outline

I. Sergei Vasilievich Rachmaninoff (1873–1943) was one of the greatest pianists of his generation. His hands were unusually large, with exceptionally long thumbs. He was a prodigy, with the ability to sight-read and almost instantly memorize any music. He impressed everyone he met while studying in Moscow at the conservatory, including Tchaikovsky, whom Rachmaninoff claimed was the single greatest influence on his compositional development.

   A. Among the works Rachmaninoff composed during his last year at the Moscow Conservatory was a piano concerto in F# minor. He later revised the concerto, and it is this revised version that we hear today when his Piano Concerto no. 1 is performed. Even in its revised version, though, it gives us an idea of Rachmaninoff's stunning precocity as a composer and helps us to understand why he so dazzled his classmates and teachers at the conservatory.

B. Rachmaninoff composed four piano concerti, among many other works. It is his piano music in general and his piano concerti in particular that are his greatest claim to compositional fame. Like Chopin before him, Rachmaninoff was a piano composer first—the piano was his musical alter ego.

C. The piano concerti offer a perfect cross-section of Rachmaninoff's musical style and expressive priorities, which were, as we have mentioned, influenced by the music of Tchaikovsky and exhibit "intensely lyric melodies; broad, sweeping gestures; rich harmony; colorful use of the piano; and powerful climax points. A profound predilection for the minor mode casts a strong melancholy shadow across most of his compositions" (Roeder, p. 301).

D. Rachmaninoff found his mature musical voice at virtually the beginning of his career, and he never substantially departed from it. This is one of the reasons that the academic community does not take his music seriously: Having achieved a generally popular, somewhat cloying musical style early in his career, he remained content to write the same sort of music, using the same sort of musical devices, for the remainder of his career, immune from the innovations of such contemporaries as Debussy, Stravinsky, Schönberg, and Bartok. But why should we deny ourselves the intense pleasures of Rachmaninoff's piano concerti, in particular, the second and third, because he managed to find his mature compositional voice before his 20th birthday?

II. The first piano concerto (1891, revised 1917) is a traditionally structured, three-movement concerto. It was published, with Tchaikovsky's assistance, in 1893, when Rachmaninoff was 20 years old and, thus, bears the designation of opus 1.

A. The third movement, marked *allegro vivace* ("fast and lively"), is in three-part, A–B–A form. As we listen to the opening A section in its entirety, let us be aware of three points:

1. The piano part is insanely difficult—the pianist is everywhere on the keyboard at once.

2. There is a tremendous degree of interplay between the orchestra and the piano, so that despite the virtuosity of the piano part, this is real concertato-style writing.

       3. This is amazingly assured music for a 19-year-old composer, whatever revisions he may subsequently have made. **Musical selection:** Rachmaninoff, Piano Concerto no. 1 in F# Minor, op. 1, movement 3, A, and B, opening.

  B. Not since Chopin, had a composer made such an auspicious debut with a concerto at such a tender age. It is a marvelous piece that is, unfortunately, rarely heard, overshadowed as it is by the second and third concerti.

  C. With regard to Rachmaninoff's piano playing, Harold Schonberg, music critic at the *New York Times*, heard Rachmaninoff play and described his technique: "He played with a minimum of physical exertion, brooding over the keys. From his fingers came an indescribable tone: warm, projecting into every corner of the hall, capable of infinite modulation…melodies were outlines with radiant authority; counterbalancing inner voices were brought out [with crystal clarity]. And those marvelous fingers seemed incapable of striking a wrong note" (Schonberg, *Lives*, pp. 522–523).

III. Rachmaninoff was such a prodigious pianist, who concertized so tirelessly until the end of his life, that it is easy to forget that more than anything else, he considered himself a composer. A traumatic event, however, almost caused him to give up composing entirely. It had a direct bearing on the creation of his Piano Concerto no. 2 in C Minor.

  A. In 1895, Rachmaninoff completed his first symphony. The symphony is the most prestigious genre of orchestral music, and a composer's first symphony represents his or her desire to be taken seriously. A first symphony is, therefore, a risk for a composer.

  B. Rachmaninoff's first symphony, in my opinion, is not just the best of his three symphonies but arguably the best Russian symphony composed between Tchaikovsky and Shostakovich. Unfortunately, that was not the opinion of the audience at the premiere, which took place on March 27, 1897. The symphony was conducted by Alexander Glazunov, a superb pianist and composer and a famous teacher but among the worst conductors to ever have picked up a baton. The premiere was a disaster, and the audience concluded that the fault lay with the composer, not the conductor.

  C. Rachmaninoff was so depressed by this experience that he became incapable of composing, until, in January of 1900, he began hypnosis therapy with a Dr. Nicholas Dahl. The treatment worked. In May of 1901, Rachmaninoff completed his second piano concerto, which he dedicated to Dr. Dahl.

D. The themes are the essence of the Piano Concerto no. 2 in C Minor. Rachmaninoff treats them in a Russian manner: as the core of the piece. This is the antithesis of the German approach, in which themes are a resource for reconstruing, recombining, fragmenting, and reassembling across the span of a movement.

E. In the first-movement sonata form, theme 1 begins with a brief introduction played by the piano that immediately establishes a serious, almost melodramatic mood: A series of sententious harmonies, built on the lowest F on the keyboard, are followed by dramatic, rippling arpeggios in anticipation of theme 1. **Musical selection:** Piano Concerto no. 2 in C Minor, op. 18, movement 1, introduction.

　1. Theme 1 enters, heavy, passionate, Slavic in tone, and in C minor. It is initially heard low in the strings, giving it the dramatic, masculine quality of a Russian baritone or bass singer. The melody itself is vocally conceived, consisting of mostly adjacent scale steps and very few leaps. Rippling piano arpeggios continue in the accompaniment. **Musical selection:** Piano Concerto no. 2 in C Minor, op. 18, movement 1, theme 1, phrases a and a^1.

　2. The third phrase of theme 1 (b) is lengthy and rhapsodic and rising in contour, under which continue the roiling piano arpeggios. Finally, the piano plays the fourth and finale phrase of the theme (b^1) and, for the first time since the concerto began, the heaviness that has characterized the music begins to give way to a lighter, brighter lyricism. **Musical selection:** Piano Concerto no. 2 in C Minor, op. 18, movement 1, theme 1, phrases b and b^1.

F. A brief modulating bridge connects to theme 2, a lyric theme in Eb major with six component phrases. In the opening phrases, a and a^1, the piano takes the lead. **Musical selection:** Piano Concerto no. 2 in C Minor, op. 18, movement 1, theme 2, phrases a and a^1.

　1. The next two phrases consist, first, of a rhapsodic extension of the theme in the strings and piano, followed by a return to the original thematic material in the piano. **Musical selection:**

Piano Concerto no. 2 in C Minor, op. 18, movement 1, theme 2, phrases b and a^2.

   2. Another contrasting phrase follows, after which the opening of the theme delicately returns, lengthened and elaborated in the piano and various solo winds. **Musical selection:** Piano Concerto no. 2 in C Minor, op. 18, movement 1, theme 2, phrases c and a^3.
   3. The subsequent cadence material and development section together take up less time in performance than either of the themes.
   4. When theme 1 returns in the recapitulation, it is aggressive and march-like, with the brass and strings initially playing the theme against a strident countermelody in the piano. **Musical selection:** Piano Concerto no. 2 in C Minor, op. 18, movement 1, recapitulation, theme 1.
   5. The second theme, on its return, is played by a solo horn over quivering strings. The mood is calm, almost surreal. **Musical selection:** Piano Concerto no. 2 in C Minor, op. 18, movement 1, recapitulation, theme 2.

G. The first movement is about its themes—developmental and transitional music are of secondary importance.

H. The second movement is a haunting nocturne and is essentially monothematic, based as it is on a single, quiet, mysterious theme, initially played by a solo clarinet. **Musical selection:** Piano Concerto no. 2 in C Minor, op. 18, movement 2, theme.
   1. The overall effect of the second movement is of a single, continuous, ever-shifting theme. The only break in the continuity is for the one and only cadenza in the concerto. An ascending piano passage and an explosive orchestral exclamation precede an ever-so-brief cadenza. Then, a gentle duet between the piano and a solo flute brings the music back down to Earth in preparation for one last playing of the main theme. **Musical selection:** Piano Concerto no. 2 in C Minor, op. 18, movement 2.
   2. The final two minutes of this movement represents some of the most beautiful and ethereal music in the repertoire.

I. The third movement (sort of sonata form) is marked *allegro scherzando* ("fast and playfully"), and it introduces a degree of exuberance that is new to the concerto. The introduction features a quiet but frisky dialogue between the low and high strings that builds up to an explosive climax. **Musical selection:** Piano Concerto no. 2 in C Minor, op. 18, movement 3, introduction, part 1.

1. A preening, macho-man piano ripples up and down, after which a pulsing, march-like orchestral passage anticipates the entry of theme 1. **Musical selection:** Piano Concerto no. 2 in C Minor, op. 18, movement 3, introduction, parts 2 and 3.
2. Theme 1 bursts out of the gate with the piano in the lead. It is a vigorous, mock-dramatic theme, based on the same motives that have powered pretty much all of the themes heard thus far in the concerto. A rhapsodic solo piano episode concludes the theme. **Musical selection:** Piano Concerto no. 2 in C Minor, op. 18, movement 3, theme 1.
3. Theme 2 is the ultimate example of Romantic-era schmaltz; this lyric, Slavic theme is played first by the violas and oboes, then by the piano. **Musical selection:** Piano Concerto no. 2 in C Minor, op. 18, movement 3, theme 2.
4. In 1946, the lyricists Buddy Kaye and Ted Mossman took this tune and added their own words, entitling the song "Full Moon and Empty Arms."
5. A brief transition leads to the development, beginning with a wild, dance-like version of theme 1. **Musical selection:** Piano Concerto no. 2 in C Minor, op. 18, movement 3, development, theme 1.
6. The recapitulation begins with theme 2; following a virtuosic episode based on the movement's introduction, it is a completely over-the-top version of theme 2 that brings the movement, and the concerto, to its conclusion. **Musical selection:** Piano Concerto no. 2 in C Minor, op. 18, movement 3, theme 2, conclusion.

IV. Rachmaninoff composed his Piano Concerto no. 3 in D Minor for his first American concert tour. He premiered the work on November 28, 1909, with the New York Symphony, conducted by Walter Damrosch. The performance went well, but the real triumph came two weeks later, when Rachmaninoff performed the concerto again, this time with the New York Philharmonic under the baton of its new conductor, Gustav Mahler.

A. In its handling of transitions, developments, harmony, form, and the piano, Rachmaninoff's third piano concerto shows a composer in total command.

B. As an example of the "Rach Three," we turn to the first theme of the first-movement sonata form. The theme is a long, folk-like melody presented directly—even simply—over a murmuring accompaniment in winds and strings. Rachmaninoff told the musicologist Joseph Yasser that the pianist must sing this theme "as a singer would sing it" (Steinberg, p. 364). **Musical selection:** Rachmaninoff, Piano Concerto no. 3 in D Minor, op. 30, movement 1, theme 1.

C. From such simple beginnings come some of the most virtuosic developments. The development section of this first movement is one of the most remarkable in the repertoire.

    1. During the course of the development—a very skillfully wrought development—the music dies away to almost nothing, as shivering string tremolos accompany bleak, isolated chords in the piano. Then begins one of the longest and most supremely difficult cadenzas in the repertoire.

    2. The placement of the cadenza in the development section is not new—we observed such cadenzas in the concerti of Mendelssohn and Tchaikovsky—but what Rachmaninoff does during the course of the cadenza *is* new and stunning. The piano by itself begins the recapitulation by playing a chordal version of theme 1. There follows a modulating bridge, in which a flute, then an oboe, then a clarinet, and then a horn play fragments of theme 1 over rippling piano arpeggios. Then, the solo piano embarks on a long, rhapsodic version of theme 2. Finally, horns and bassoons enter, and the cadenza, and the recapitulation with it, comes to its conclusion.

    3. The coda follows, with the piano and orchestra playing theme 1 as it was originally heard, after which the movement comes to a rapid and surprisingly quiet conclusion. **Musical selection:** Rachmaninoff, Piano Concerto no. 3 in D Minor, op. 30, movement 1, cadenza and conclusion.

V. Rachmaninoff's fourth piano concerto has not found a permanent place in the repertoire, but his final work for piano and orchestra, the Rhapsody on a Theme of Paganini, op. 43, of 1934 most definitely has.

This work, which lies outside the purview of this course because it is not, technically, a concerto, is considered by many to be Rachmaninoff's greatest work for piano and orchestra.

Lecture Seventeen
The Russian Concerto, Part 1

Scope: Alexander Glazunov, who reconciled 19th-century Russian musical nationalism with German compositional style, is the foundation on which this examination of the Russian concerto is based. As a composer and music educator, he cast a shadow across the entire Russian musical scene, exerting an influence on such composers as Kabalevsky and Khachaturian. Glazunov's Violin Concerto in A Minor is virtuosic, yet the orchestral writing is rich and perfectly balanced with the solo violin. The third movement of his Piano Concerto no. 1 features a theme and variations, a rare structure in concerto literature. Although Dmitri Kabalevsky and Aram Khachaturian both conformed to Soviet cultural ideology, they managed to compose works that endured, turning to folk music for much of their inspiration. Kabalevsky's music has an "edge" that sets it apart, while Khachaturian's Piano Concerto in Db, a virtuoso work in the grand tradition, is considered the greatest piano concerto to come out of the Soviet Union.

Outline

I. Rachmaninoff's concerti mark the end of an era that began in the 1820s and 1830s with the concerti of Paganini and Liszt—the era of the Romantic virtuoso concerto. By 1934, when Rachmaninoff composed his Rhapsody on a Theme of Paganini, entirely new approaches to the language of music and musical expression had evolved. The next two lectures focus on concerti written between 1904 and 1964 by the Russian composers Glazunov, Khachaturian, Kabalevsky, Prokofiev and Shostakovich. These concerti span the musicological and ideological divide between pre-Soviet and Soviet Russia.

II. Alexander Konstantinovich Glazunov was born in St. Petersburg in 1865 and died in Paris in 1936. A prodigious talent, he became the protégé of Nikolai Rimsky-Korsakov, the youngest and most talented member of the group of leading nationalist Russian composers known as the "Russian Five." As a composer and music educator, Glazunov cast a shadow across the entire Russian musical scene.

A. In 1899, Glazunov was appointed professor of composition and orchestration at the St. Petersburg Conservatory, and in 1905, he became director of the conservatory, holding the post for 25 years, through World War I, the Russian Revolution and Civil War, Lenin's rule, and the first two years of Stalin's first Five-Year Plan.

B. Today, Glazunov is recognized as the single composer who finally reconciled 19th-century musical nationalism with the developmental techniques of German compositional style. He is the foundation on which our entire examination of the Russian concerto is based. He oversaw the educations of both Prokofiev and Shostakovich and influenced the music of Dmitri Kabalevsky and Aram Khachaturian, among many others.

C. Glazunov was a musical polymath: an excellent pianist, with a perfect ear; the ability to sight-read anything; a prodigious musical memory; and a comprehensive knowledge of music history and compositional technique. He was also one of those rare individuals who could play almost any orchestral instrument.

D. Glazunov composed five concerti: one for violin, two for piano, one for alto saxophone, and a *Concerto Ballata* for orchestra and 'cello. For the first half of his career, Glazunov concentrated on writing symphonies and completed eight of them by the time he was 41 years old. In 1910, he began his ninth symphony but abandoned it after completing the first movement. He never wrote another symphonic movement again. Instead, he focused on writing concerti.

E. Glazunov's Violin Concerto in A Minor was written in 1904. It is cast in three continuous movements.
  1. Like Tchaikovsky's violin concerto, Glazunov's can be knuckle-bustingly virtuosic, but it leaves the impression of glorious lyricism—another example of the enduring vision of the violin as coloratura voice.
  2. Although this concerto is about the solo violin, Glazunov's orchestral writing is rich, varied, colorful, and perfectly balanced with the solo violin.
  3. Glazunov wrote this work for Leopold Auer, who premiered it in 1905.

F. The first movement (*moderato*) begins with a brief, throbbing introduction in the orchestra, followed by a long, Slavic-sounding theme in the home key of A minor. **Musical selection:** Glazunov, Violin Concerto in A Minor, op. 82, movement 1, opening.

G. The first movement merges seamlessly into the second, which begins in the key of C# major. Note the rich and resonant opening of this movement, played as it is, on the solo violin's lowest string—the G string. **Musical selection:** Glazunov, Violin Concerto in A Minor, op. 82, movement 2, opening.

H. The third-movement rondo in A major is just fantastic: over-the-top exuberant, brilliantly colored, and as virtuosic as anything in the repertoire. One of the most extraordinary things about the movement is the way in which Glazunov balances the solo violin with the constantly shifting orchestral textures and combinations he creates during the movement. **Musical selection:** Glazunov, Violin Concerto in A Minor, op. 82, movement 3 in its entirety.

I. Glazunov's Piano Concerto no. 1 of 1911 has but two movements, the second of which is cast in theme and variations form, a structure rarely encountered in concerto literature. What makes Glazunov's movement special, though, is that over the course of the movement's nine variations, he manages to make this one movement sound like three.

  1. The theme and first four variations are slow, creating the effect of a slow movement. Variations five through seven are fast–slow–fast in tempo, which together create the effect of a scherzo. The final variations (eight and nine) take on the character of a finale. **Musical selections:** Glazunov, Piano Concerto no. 1 in F Minor, op. 92, movement 2, opening, and movement 2, conclusion.

  2. I have always thought of Glazunov as the "Russian Brahms," a composer whose music is always beautifully crafted, uncompromising, and truly written from the heart.

III. Glazunov was 49 years old at the start of World War I. In 1917, the Russian Revolution broke out as a result of the criminal ineptitude of Russia's leadership. After the tsar was forced to abdicate, Lenin and the Bolsheviks began their political campaign, ultimately bringing down the provisional government and achieving a coup that had them firmly in power by early 1918.

A. Then began a civil war between the Bolsheviks (the Reds) and the anti-Bolsheviks (the Whites) that ravaged Russia until 1920. By that year, Russia was nearly destroyed and its people were starving. Much of the cream of the musical establishment left Russia for the more hospitable climes of the West, resulting in a musical gap that would not be closed in the Soviet Union until the composers and performers born just after the turn of the 20th century had matured.

B. The artistic environment in the mid- and late 1920s was very different from that under the tsar. The arts had been co-opted by the state to legitimize the new Soviet society. Because of the abstract nature of instrumental music, the Soviet bureaucracy had a difficult time figuring out what was "appropriate," which for a few years at least, gave composers a bit more expressive freedom than their fellow artists.

C. That freedom did not last long.
  1. In 1932, four years into the first of Stalin's Five-Year Plans, the Union of Soviet Composers was created. The "union" was nothing of the sort; it was an iron-fisted committee, established to monitor and control the content of all music produced in the Soviet Union.
  2. All music was required to display "socialist realism": It had to portray and glorify the Communist Party and its ideology; it had to be accessible to the masses and, therefore, had to include folk or folk-like music; and it had to exclude modern, Western musical languages, which were declared to be decadent and "bourgeois."
  3. In January of 1936, the best and brightest star in the Soviet musical firmament, Dmitri Shostakovich, was condemned for his opera *Lady Macbeth*. Now, no one was safe.
  4. Another round of condemnations and purges followed in 1948 and 1949. Stalin died in 1953, and slowly, Soviet restrictions on music were relaxed. But it was not until 1985, with the advent of *glasnost* ("openness") and, later, *perestroika* ("restructuring"), that Soviet composers were allowed to experiment with once-forbidden expressive content and compositional techniques.
  5. Of the hundreds of composers who lived and worked in the Soviet Union, four composed music that managed to

transcend the absurd constraints of Soviet socialist realism: Shostakovich, Prokofiev, Kabalevsky, and Khachaturian. The latter two managed to write enduring music, despite the fact that they toed the party line.

IV. Dmitri Borisovich Kabalevsky (1904–1987) apparently never wrote a note of music until his early 20s and still managed to learn the craft and leave behind a substantial body of work.

   A. Kabalevsky was the quintessential Soviet *apparatchik*. He became a charter member of the Moscow branch of the Union of Soviet Composers when it was established in 1932 and a full professor at the Moscow Conservatory in 1939, and he joined the Communist Party in 1940. He was on the Soviet Committee for the Defense of Peace, and as a high-profile member of the Society for the Promotion of Friendship, he traveled abroad frequently, something that only the most politically trustworthy Soviet artists were allowed to do.

   B. Kabalevsky composed six concerti: three for piano, two for 'cello, and one for violin. The 'Cello Concerto no. 2, composed in 1964, is typical of Kabalevsky's music in its use of melodic and rhythmic elements drawn from Russian folk music, and it employs the officially approved tonal harmonic language of socialist realism. But it has a rhythmic power, a melodic and harmonic edge, and a structural integrity that separate it from the pack.

   1. The concerto is set in three movements, but Kabalevsky puts a twist on the expected tempi of each movement: Instead of fast–slow–fast, the three movements follow the scheme slow–fast–slow. The second movement, marked *presto marcato* ("very fast and with emphasis"), is in my opinion, the most impressive. **Musical selection:** Kabalevsky, 'Cello Concerto no. 2, op. 77, movement 2, opening.

   2. Although this is attractive and well-written music, it conforms to the dictates of Soviet ideology and, as a result, sounds stylistically anachronistic. It does not reflect the evolving Western trends of its day. Its musical language is hardly different from that of Dvorak's 'cello concerto.

V. Like Kabalevsky, Aram Khachaturian (1903–1978) toed the Communist Party line. Like Kabalevsky's music, Khachaturian's draws heavily on folk music for its rhythmic and melodic substance—in

Khachaturian's case, from Armenia. However, Khachaturian did not succeed in avoiding condemnation from the Central Committee of the Communist Party.

A. Khachaturian wrote three concerti: a piano concerto in 1936, a violin concerto in 1940, and a 'cello concerto in 1946. The piano concerto is one of the best piano concerti of the 20th century and is considered the single greatest piano concerto to come out of the Soviet Union. It is a work in the grand virtuoso tradition.

    1. The first-movement sonata form is marked *allegro non troppo e maestoso* ("fast, but not too fast and majestically"). The most majestic theme 1 appears in the piano after a brief but craggy—almost Stravinskian—orchestral introduction. **Musical selection:** Khachaturian, Piano Concerto in Db Major, movement 1, introduction and theme 1.

    2. The second theme is folk-inspired and makes its appearance in the oboe. **Musical selection:** Khachaturian, Piano Concerto in Db Major, movement 1, theme 2.

B. Khachaturian, here, shows himself to be the prototypical post-Romantic, post-Glazunov Soviet composer: He was not an innovator but, rather, a culminator, whose music combines almost perfectly the state-sanctioned, folk-dominated, Soviet-realist style with instrumental virtuosity and a first-rate compositional technique.

C. The third-movement finale features a thrilling, vaguely jazzy conclusion. **Musical selection:** Khachaturian, Piano Concerto in Db Major, movement 3, conclusion.

D. Khachaturian's music deserves much more in-depth examination than we've had the opportunity to give it here. We might dare to call him "a Soviet composer for all of us."

Lecture Eighteen
The Russian Concerto, Part 2

Scope: Sergei Prokofiev had a wry and acerbic personality that found its way into his music. He viewed the piano as a percussion instrument, to be hammered rather than stroked. His machine-age compositional style produced music of explosive rhythmic momentum and great structural clarity, with volatile harmonic shifts and brilliant virtuosity. But he could write music of enormous lyrical beauty as well, as manifested by the opening of his Piano Concerto no. 3 in C Major, a trademark work whose popularity made him a living for years. In this lecture, we discuss, along with Piano Concerto no. 3, Prokofiev's Piano Concerto no. 1 in Db Major, a precocious, fast-paced work that exhibits brilliant pianism, and we also look at his Violin Concerto no. 2 in G Minor, a work designed for performance in the Soviet Union and, therefore, less idiosyncratic than the two piano concerti. Like Prokofiev, Dmitri Shostakovich owed much to his Russian roots, but his music also shows the influence of Mahler, Berg, and Stravinsky—an influence he did not try to hide from the Soviet authorities, who typically condemned all things Western. Although Shostakovich wrote all his music under Soviet rule, he was periodically attacked by the authorities for writing music that did not conform to the ideology of Soviet socialist realism. His music is often intensely personal, filled with humor, satire, inside jokes, rage, despair, and even violence. In this lecture, we examine his Piano Concerto no. 1 in C Minor, Piano Concerto no. 2 in F Major, Violin Concerto no. 1 in A Minor, and 'Cello Concerto no. 1 in Eb Major.

Outline

I. In 1918, Sergei Prokofiev (1891–1953) left Russia before the Russian Civil War nearly destroyed the country. He scandalized the Russian émigré community when he decided to return to Russia, which had become the Soviet Union, in 1936. Initially, Prokofiev was thrilled to be home. He was honored and celebrated and even allowed to travel abroad. But the good times did not last long. After 1937, he was no longer allowed to leave the country. In 1948, he was censured by the Soviet government, accused of writing music "marked with formal perversions alien to the Soviet people." He died a broken man in 1953, about one hour before Stalin died.

A. Prokofiev was a spectacular prodigy, both as composer and pianist. At the age of 23, he received the St. Petersburg Conservatory's Rubinstein Prize, the highest award available to a pianist, for performing his own Piano Concerto no. 1.

B. Frank to a fault, Prokofiev had an acerbic personality that many found alienating. He was an anti-Romantic who claimed to despise the music of Liszt and Chopin and who saw the piano as, first and foremost, a percussion instrument.

C. Prokofiev's Piano Concerto no. 1 in Db Major, op. 10, of 1912 is cast as a single 15-minute-long movement, divided into four large sections.

1. The concerto opens with a grand series of broadly spaced Db-major chords, immediately followed by theme 1, played first by the piano and the orchestra, then by the orchestra alone. **Musical selection:** Prokofiev, Piano Concerto no. 1 in Db Major, op. 10, part 1, theme 1.

2. The piano immediately embarks on an absolutely incendiary modulating bridge, first alone, then quietly accompanied by the orchestra. **Musical selection:** Prokofiev, Piano Concerto no. 1 in Db Major, op. 10, part 1, modulating bridge.

3. This is pianism unlike anything we have heard in this course: The sound of the piano must be metallic, not warm; hammered, not bel canto. This is machine-age music, powerfully influenced by the same fast-paced, early-20th-century environment that so affected Stravinsky and Schönberg, Kokoschka, and the Italian futurists.

4. The piano next plays a brief second theme; a development section of sorts follows, then theme 1 returns and brings this first section of the concerto to its conclusion. **Musical selection:** Prokofiev, Piano Concerto no. 1 in Db Major, op. 10, part 1, conclusion.

5. The second part of the concerto opens with a mysterious and gentle theme initially scored for strings. **Musical selection:** Prokofiev, Piano Concerto no. 1 in Db Major, op. 10, part 2, opening.

©2006 The Teaching Company.

6. A series of repeated chords in the orchestra begins the playful and most virtuosic third part of the concerto. **Musical selection:** Prokofiev, Piano Concerto no. 1 in Db Major, op. 10, part 3, opening.
7. The fourth and final part of the concerto begins relatively quietly. **Musical selection:** Prokofiev, Piano Concerto no. 1 in Db Major, op. 10, part 4, opening.
8. The concerto rapidly gains momentum, until at the end, the opening theme of part 1 returns, bringing the concerto to a clangorous conclusion. **Musical selection:** Prokofiev, Piano Concerto no. 1 in Db Major, op. 10, part 4, conclusion.

D. Prokofiev's third piano concerto (1921) became his musical calling card, with which he thrilled audiences and made his living for years. As we did with his first piano concerto, we will focus on the major thematic and formal features of each movement, so that we might have a sense of the larger structural flow when listening to the concerto in its entirety.
   1. The opening of the first movement is one of the most sensational in the entire concerto repertoire. Prokofiev begins the concerto with a slow, seductive Russian tune, played initially by a solo clarinet. **Musical selection:** Prokofiev, Piano Concerto no. 3 in C Major, op. 26, movement 1, introduction.
   2. This ethereal tune becomes the basis for theme 1, which now explodes out of the box. **Musical selection:** Prokofiev, Piano Concerto no. 3 in C Major, op. 26, movement 1, theme 1, opening.
   3. This is vintage Prokofiev: Turn-on-a-dime harmonic shifts and the most brilliant pianism combine to create an excitement level more common to rock 'n roll than to concert music.
   4. Theme 2, presented initially by a solo oboe and accompanied by pizzicato violins and castanets, has a certain acerbic, comic quality to it, rather like Prokofiev himself. **Musical selection:** Prokofiev, Piano Concerto no. 3 in C Major, op. 26, movement 1, theme 2.
   5. The exposition concludes with an impassioned version of the gorgeous folk-inspired introduction that began the movement. **Musical selection:** Prokofiev, Piano Concerto no. 3 in C Major, op. 26, movement 1, cadence material.

6. The development section is rich and lyric, rather than energized and metallic. This changes when the retransition powers the music into the recapitulation. **Musical selection:** Prokofiev, Piano Concerto no. 3 in C Major, op. 26, movement 1, retransition and recapitulation, themes 1 and 2.
7. The movement concludes with the same knuckle-busting music Prokofiev used for the retransition. **Musical selection:** Prokofiev, Piano Concerto no. 3 in C Major, op. 26, movement 1, coda.
8. The second movement consists of a theme and five variations. The theme is a quirky, sort of slow 18th-century gavotte as interpreted by an early-20th-century Russian modernist composer. **Musical selection:** Prokofiev, Piano Concerto no. 3 in C Major, op. 26, movement 2, theme, opening.
9. The form of the episodic third movement can be schematicized as A–B–C–A, plus coda: A bouncing, angular theme A is followed by a swirling theme B, which is followed by a long, broad, genuinely Romantic theme, followed by a return to theme A. The coda brings all together in a dazzling display of virtuosity. **Musical selection:** Prokofiev, Piano Concerto no. 3 in C Major, op. 26, movement 3, coda.
10. Prokofiev's formal structure, piano writing, and wonderful and quirky themes are tight as a drum. The concerto's wry and brilliant personality marks it as Prokofiev's own. Only Bela Bartok will produce concerti of like structural clarity and pure, rhythmic power.

E. Prokofiev's Violin Concerto no. 2 in G Minor, op. 63, is one of two violin concerti he wrote. At the time of its composition, in 1935, he had decided to return permanently to Soviet Russia. Thus, it is a piece of music that more or less subscribes to the rules and regulations of socialist realism: It is Classical in spirit and more lyric, less idiosyncratic than any of his previous concerti.
   1. The first-movement sonata form opens with the violin playing, unaccompanied, a lyric theme that betrays its Russian roots by its short, repetitive phrases and asymmetrical phrase structure. **Musical selection:** Prokofiev, Violin Concerto no. 2 in G Minor, op. 63, movement 1, theme 1, opening.
   2. The second movement opens with a gentle, serenade-like theme heard over a guitar-like accompaniment in the

orchestra. **Musical selection:** Prokofiev, Violin Concerto no. 2 in G Minor, op. 63, movement 2, opening.
3. The third-movement finale is a raucous dance, but with a hint of the sort of "grotesquerie" for which Prokofiev had been so well known to this point in his career. **Musical selection:** Prokofiev, Violin Concerto no. 2 in G Minor, op. 63, movement 3, opening.
4. The concerto concludes with what sounds like vintage Prokofiev. **Musical selection:** Prokofiev, Violin Concerto no. 2 in G Minor, op. 63, movement 3, conclusion.
5. It would seem that, compositionally, there are two Prokofiev's, each of them a composer of genius: one trying to find his way in the West, and the other trying to find his way at home. They are not mutually exclusive, but complementary.

II. Unlike Prokofiev, Shostakovich (1906–1975) had no choice about being a Soviet artist. He lived his entire creative life under the thumb of the Communist Party. (For an in-depth look at the life, work, and times of Dmitri Shostakovich, see Professor Greenberg's Teaching Company course *Great Masters: Shostakovich—His Life and Music*.)

A. Although both Prokofiev's and Shostakovich's music is rooted in its Russian heritage, it is the music of Shostakovich that continues to show the influence of Mahler, Berg, and Stravinsky. Shostakovich lived his life at the artistic edge. His artistic proclivities caused him untold misery. He trod the thinnest of lines, explaining the meaning of his music in one way in public and in an entirely different way in private.

B. Shostakovich was the most important composer of symphonies and string quartets in the 20th century. His six concerti are not at quite the same level, but they are superb works, nevertheless.

C. Shostakovich's first piano concerto, composed in 1933, is a crisp neo-Classic work in four movements. It features a solo trumpet, which at times, takes center stage, even, for example, at the very end of the concerto.
1. At that fourth-movement conclusion, the orchestra reaches a climax and sets up the brilliant piano cadenza, which eventually merges into the main theme of the movement. Suddenly, the trumpet interrupts with a fanfare; the piano tries to brush it aside by playing a crazed bit of polka music, but

the trumpet ultimately prevails and leads the movement, and the concerto, to its conclusion. **Musical selection:** Shostakovich, Piano Concerto no. 1 in C Minor, op. 35, movement 4, conclusion.
    2. This is superbly written concertato-styled music: confrontational, humorous, satirical, and in all ways, theatrical.

D. Shostakovich's second piano concerto was composed 24 years after the first, in 1957. It was written for Shostakovich's son Maxim, who premiered it on his 19th birthday on May 10, 1957. The work is filled with flash and energy and all sorts of inside jokes.
    1. One of these jokes is a reference to exercise no. 2 from Charles Hanon's *The Virtuoso Pianist*, a compendium of 60 graded exercises published in 1900 that has become the bane of almost every piano student since that time. **Piano example:** Hanon, Exercise no. 2, opening.
    2. In Shostakovich's marvelous send-up of the Hanon exercise, the piano twists and turns and starts over and over again as it tries to "get it right." **Musical selection:** Piano Concerto no. 2 in F Major, op. 102, movement 3, Hanon quote.
    3. The movement and the concerto conclude with a like passage, only now, the timpani, like some pitiless and incompetent piano teacher, beats time for the piano but on the wrong beats. **Musical selection:** Piano Concerto no. 2 in F Major, op. 102, movement 3, conclusion.

E. Shostakovich dedicated both of his violin concerti, completed in 1948 and 1967, to the Russian violinist David Oistrakh (1908–1974). Where Shostakovich's piano concerti are short and generally playful works, the violin concerti are long and most serious.
    1. Shostakovich was halfway through composing Violin Concerto no. 1 in A Minor when, on February 10, 1948, the Central Committee of the Communist Party brought charges against him, Sergei Prokofiev, and Aram Khachaturian, among others, accusing them of "formalism" and "antidemocratic tendencies" and of writing music that evoked the style of Western "modernist bourgeois" composers.

2. Shostakovich's violin concerto bears witness to his fury and his helplessness. He did not release the work until 1955, two years after Stalin's death. The second-movement scherzo bears witness to Shostakovich's rage and sense of hopelessness. This is the kind of music that the Soviets condemned as "formalism." It has nothing to do with socialist realism and everything to do with anguished personal expression. **Musical selection:** Shostakovich, Violin Concerto no. 1 in A Minor, op. 77 (op. 99), movement 2, opening.

F. Shostakovich composed both of his 'cello concerti for the great Russian 'cellist and conductor Mstislav Rostropovich. Dating from 1959 and 1966, they are, like the violin concerti, dark, powerful, and intensely personal works. We will hear the exposition of the sonata-form first movement of 'Cello Concerto no. 1 in Eb Major, op. 107. This is edgy, intense, deeply self-expressive music—again, not the sort of music that would fall under the heading of Soviet socialist realism. **Musical selection:** Shostakovich, 'Cello Concerto no. 1 in Eb Major, op. 107, movement 1, exposition.

G. Most of Shostakovich's most haunting, violent, and personal music was heard only after Stalin's death, when it finally became possible in the Soviet Union—although only for an artist of Shostakovich's stature—to personally express himself.

Lecture Nineteen
The Concerto in France

Scope: The works of Maurice Ravel, Jacques Ibert, François Poulenc, and Henri Dutilleux are all, to some degree or another, profoundly influenced by the French language. In musical terms, this means a predilection for sound for its own sake; a penchant for long, sometimes languorous melodies; a tendency toward slow harmonic turnover; and a greater emphasis on thematic variation than on thematic development. Maurice Ravel wrote two concerti that are generally considered the two outstanding French concerti of the 20th century: the Piano Concerto in G Major and the Concerto in D Major for Left Hand. Jacques Ibert's Flute Concerto reflects the French predilection for wind instruments, with their diverse and subtle timbres. The work is rightly considered one of the finest wind concerti in the repertoire. François Poulenc, once considered a lightweight composer, is now seen as the most important composer between Ravel and Olivier Messiaen. In this lecture, we discuss his wonderful Piano Concerto of 1949. The music of Henri Dutilleux is rarely heard in the United States, but every piece he has written is superb, including his 'Cello Concerto, which we discuss in this lecture.

Outline

I. The essential aspect of French music that differentiates it from other musical traditions is the overwhelming degree to which it reflects not just the character but also the essence of the French language.

  A. The French language is about vowels and combinations of vowels that create complex and often tongue-twisting constructs called *diphthongs*. The consonants in French are not guttural as in German and English but, rather, smooth and understated. The overall effect is a language characterized by color, subtlety, nuance, and continuity, rather than by sharpness of articulation, discontinuity, and harshness.

  B. The degree to which the French language, as the spiritual essence of French culture, has manifested itself in the French arts, philosophy, cuisine, and design is astonishing. In France, style and

substance are not separable. In terms of French music, this means that:
1. Sonority is as important as melody, harmony, and rhythm.
2. Melodies conceived by native French-speaking composers tend to be long and often languorous compared with melodies by German composers.
3. Chord changes occur more slowly than in Italian and German music.
4. The sort of development that we have been witness to in German music is less important than thematic variation, something that French music has in common with Russian music.

C. From the late 18th century through the mid-19th, the focus of attention in French music was on opera—lyric theater, as the French preferred to call it. It was not until the 20th century that French composers made a significant contribution to the genre of concerto. We focus on four of these composers in this lecture: Maurice Ravel, Jacques Ibert, François Poulenc, and Henri Dutilleux. Their music will exhibit, in different ways and to different degrees, those aspects of French music that we have just observed.

II. Maurice Ravel (1875–1937) inherited his love of precision from his Swiss father and his love of Spanish music from his mother, who was a native Basque. He studied at the Paris Conservatory, completing his studies as a composition protégé of Gabriel Fauré.

A. Ravel experienced success long before he graduated from the conservatory. His music began to be regularly published and performed in 1898, and by the time he left the conservatory in 1905, he had written a number of genuine masterworks, including the piano piece *Jeux d'eau* and his String Quartet in F Major.

B. Ravel's teacher, Fauré, encouraged his already marked predilection to write music that broke the rules of harmony and counterpoint so dear to the directors of the conservatory. As a result, Ravel never received any of the prizes so coveted by the students and so important for their future success. These included the prestigious *Prix de Rome*. By 1905, Ravel was famous and considered, along with Claude Debussy, the most important young composer in France. The conservatory directors' failure to recognize Ravel's compositional achievements created a public scandal— *L'Affaire Ravel*. Ultimately, the head of the conservatory was forced to resign and his place was taken by Fauré.

C. The names of Maurice Ravel and Claude Debussy are constantly linked as the two most representative French "Impressionist" composers of the early 20th century. Ravel had tremendous respect for Debussy, although Debussy was not particularly kind to Ravel. (Debussy was constitutionally incapable of saying anything nice about anyone.)

  1. Neither composer stole from the other. Like Leibniz and Newton, who almost simultaneously discovered calculus, Ravel and Debussy arrived at much the same artistic place at the same time by cultivating in their music the French predilections for diphthong and color, for blurred musical edges and "sound" (*sonority*) for its own sake.

  2. The difference between the two composers was that Debussy was a radical modernist who continued to experiment musically to the end of his life, whereas Ravel was content to work within a compositional language that never broke with traditional tonal harmony. Sadly, Debussy composed no concerti, but Ravel composed two, working on them simultaneously between 1929 and 1931. They are generally considered the two outstanding French concerti of the 20th century.

D. Ravel's Piano Concerto in G Major (1931) is a three-movement work that reflects the composer's infatuation with both Spanish music and jazz. He heard jazz extensively during a tour of Canada and the United States in 1927 and 1928.

  1. The opening of the first-movement sonata form also demonstrates Ravel's fascination with clocks, mechanical gadgets, and toys. As if starting some gigantic musical contraption, the movement begins with the percussionist releasing the wound-up spring of a musical whip—a so-called "slapstick." Thus triggered, a jaunty, music-box-like theme 1 is heard first in the piccolo, then in the trumpet, all the while accompanied by a chattering solo piano, which is playing in two different keys at the same time. **Musical selection:** Ravel, Piano Concerto in G Major, movement 1, theme 1.

2. Theme 2 follows immediately. This is eclectic music: The phrases played by the piano have a distinctly Spanish feel, while the wind and trumpet interludes that punctuate the piano sound like something out of George Gershwin's *Rhapsody in Blue*. **Musical selection:** Ravel, Piano Concerto in G Major, movement 1, theme 2.
3. A third theme follows, which is, in reality, a development of theme 2, bringing the exposition to its conclusion. **Musical selection:** Ravel, Piano Concerto in G Major, movement 1, theme 3.
4. A high-energy development section follows, based on theme 1 and the jazzy, Gershwin-like interlude from theme 2. As we listen to the development section and the beginning of theme 1 in the recapitulation, we should be especially aware of the collaborative nature of the relationship between the piano and the orchestra. **Musical selection:** Ravel, Piano Concerto in G Major, movement 1, development and recapitulation, opening.
5. The exquisite second movement is, according to Ravel, an homage to the slow movement of Mozart's Clarinet Quintet.
6. The third movement (*presto*) is filled with snap and humor: It has the whiz and bang of great circus music. **Musical selection:** Ravel, Piano Concerto in G Major, movement 3, opening.

E. Ravel was commissioned to write his Concerto in D Major for Left Hand by the pianist Paul Wittgenstein, brother of the philosopher Ludwig Wittgenstein. Paul had his right arm shot off when he was a soldier in the Austrian army on the Russian front during World War I. (Ravel, at age 39, tried to enlist in the French army in 1914 but was rejected as too short and underweight. He managed to be accepted as a truck driver and saw action on the western front until discharged because of ill health in 1917.)
1. The Concerto in D Major is much more in the Lisztian tradition than the Concerto in G Major, in that its solo piano part utterly dominates the piece. When you listen to this virtuosic and heroic music, it is hard to believe that the piano part is being played by the pianist's left hand alone.
2. The concerto begins with a lengthy introductory build-up in the orchestra. When the piano finally enters, we expect something magnificent and we are not disappointed. Ravel

wanted to write music worthy of Paul Wittgenstein's own heroic struggles and, in this, he succeeded mightily. **Musical selection:** Ravel, Piano Concerto in D Major for Left Hand, piano entry.

3. Paul Wittgenstein, disgusted by Austria's embrace of the Nazis, immigrated to the United States in 1938, where he lived until his death in 1961. He commissioned other left-handed works from, among other composers, Richard Strauss, Benjamin Britten, Sergei Prokofiev, and Paul Hindemith. He rightly regarded Ravel's concerto a great work.

III. Jacques Ibert (1890–1962) was a first-rate composer who wrote direct, relatively accessible, relatively traditional-sounding music in a 20th century increasingly bent on experimentation. Thus, his music might seem irrelevant to some, but it exudes an elegance, deftness of expression, Gallic charm, and a genuine *joie de vivre* that is all the more special for its rarity in the 20th century.

A. Ibert studied at the Paris Conservatory and won many prizes there. In 1919, he was awarded the *Prix de Rome* for his cantata *Le Poète et la fée*. He wrote important music in virtually every genre, including seven operas. His Flute Concerto is rightly considered among the outstanding wind concerti in the repertoire.

B. The French, traditionally, have found great appeal in the diverse and subtle colors of the woodwind choir. For example, one of the elements we identify as part of the "French style" in Baroque music is the French predilection for wind instruments. The French love of color and nuance has led French composers—more than any other national group of composers—to cultivate the woodwind quintet.

C. Ibert's Flute Concerto (1934) is cast in what by now should be the extremely familiar three-movement, fast–slow–fast scheme.

1. The first movement is a taut, compact sonata form. Despite the virtuosity of the flute part, the essentially Classical nature of the concerto is demonstrated by the collaborative relationship between the flute and the orchestra. We will listen to the entire exposition: The briefest of orchestral introductions leads to a sharply etched, perpetual-motion-type theme, played primarily by the solo flute, which is immediately followed by a slower, more lyric second theme, played entirely by the flute, and last,

a vigorous bit of cadence material shared between the flute and the orchestra. **Musical selection:** Ibert, Flute Concerto, movement 1, exposition.
   2. The mysterious second movement sees a long-breathed and lyric flute melody float above an undulating and equally lyric string accompaniment. **Musical selection:** Ibert, Flute Concerto, movement 2, opening.
   3. The third movement (*allegro scherzando*, "fast and playfully") is Paganini for the flute. **Musical selection:** Ibert, Flute Concerto, movement 3, opening.
   4. This work, along with Ibert's String Quartet of 1942 and his Trio for Violin, 'Cello and Harp of 1944, is not currently in the mainstream repertoire in the United States but should be.

IV. François Poulenc (1899–1963) is the most important French composer between Ravel and Olivier Messiaen. Yet some critics still claim that the directness, accessibility, and often burlesque theatricality of Poulenc's music disqualify him from consideration as a "serious" composer.
   A. In the following excerpt from the fifth and last of Poulenc's concerti, his Piano Concerto of 1949, we should note the following:
      1. The first movement is in three-part A–B–A form, in which moderately fast outer sections bookend a slow middle section.
      2. In the first A section, Poulenc writes a great tune; typical of all his concerti, he entirely avoids virtuosity for its own sake and, instead, involves his soloist in an ongoing dialogue with the orchestra. **Musical selection:** Poulenc, Piano Concerto, movement 1, A, opening.
      3. The slow middle section of this first movement has an almost religious, chorale-like sensibility to it. **Musical selection:** Poulenc, Piano Concerto, movement 1, B–A.
      4. Poulenc was described by Claude Rostand as "a bit of monk and a bit of hooligan." We hear both personalities in this first movement of his Piano Concerto, and it is hard to imagine a more delightful combination of musical characters.
   B. Poulenc came to fame as a member of a group of young composers known as *Les Six* ("The Six"). The others were: Arthur Honegger, Georges Auric, Louis Durey, Germaine Tailleferre, and Darius

Milhaud. What the members of *Les Six* had in common was their rejection of Romanticism and Impressionism. They wanted music that, in Poulenc's words, was "clear, healthy and robust—music, as frankly French in spirit as Stravinsky's Petrushka is Russian" (Schonberg, *Lives*, p. 474).

C. Of *Les Six*, Auric, Durey, and Tailleferre produced nothing of lasting value. Poulenc, who was thought to be nothing more than a lightweight composer, ultimately turned out to be the one who continued to develop.

D. Like the first movement, the second movement of Poulenc's Piano Concerto is a three-part, A–B–A form, with slow and lyric A sections bookending a fast, dramatic middle section. **Musical selection:** Poulenc, Piano Concerto, movement 2, A, opening.

E. Poulenc's concerto was commissioned by the Boston Symphony Orchestra and was premiered in Boston on January 6, 1950, with Poulenc at the piano under the baton of Charles Munch. Inspired by this "New World" commission and premiere, Poulenc decided to pay tribute to America by inserting into the third-movement rondo a bit of Stephen Foster's "Old Folks at Home," juxtaposed against bits of Jacques Offenbach's famous can-can music. It is a real *mélange* and a perfect and perfectly engaging reference to the enduring friendship between the United States and France. The musical "hooligan" in Poulenc led him to entitle the movement *Rondeau à la française*, and it is wonderful. **Musical selection:** Poulenc, Piano Concerto, movement 3.

V. Henri Dutilleux (b. 1916), whose music is rarely heard in the United States, studied at the Paris Conservatory and won the *Prix de Rome* in 1938. Since serving as music director for French Radio between 1945 and 1963, he has held a number of teaching positions, including professor of composition at the Paris Conservatory.

A. Dutilleux, in his desire to make each of his works as perfect as it can be, writes very slowly. The main characteristics of his compositional style include:
1. A rejection of what he calls "prefabricated scaffolding"—that is, preexisting formal structures.
2. A predilection for sonority—what Dutilleux calls "the joy of sound."
3. An economy of means.

B. It took Dutilleux more than 10 years to complete his 'Cello Concerto of 1970. The work is in five movements and subtitled *A Whole Remote World*, a line from Charles Baudelaire's poem "*La Chevelure.*" Each of the five movements is entitled with an inscription from Baudelaire, intended to indicate its mood and inspiration.

C. As an example of Dutilleux's 'Cello Concerto, we turn to the conclusion of the fourth movement and the beginning of the fifth and final movement, which is entitled "Nurse Your Dreams" and provides a ringing and fittingly dramatic conclusion to the concerto.

D. Sounding quite modern, this is hauntingly beautiful and powerful music, in which melody and the voice of the 'cello are of preeminent importance and in which the French love of nuance, color, and sound for its own sake are as operative as in any work of Ravel, Ibert, or Poulenc. **Musical selection:** Dutilleux, 'Cello Concerto, movement 4, conclusion, and movement 5, opening.

E. Dutilleux's Violin Concerto (*The Tree of Dreams*) is also a superb work and recommended listening.

Lecture Twenty
Bartok

Scope: Bartok combined melodic, harmonic, and rhythmic elements drawn from Eastern European folk music, a love for Classical-era forms, an impeccable Germanic compositional technique, and an innate sense of drama to create viscerally exciting and intellectually rewarding music. He was not a revolutionary but a synthesist. The influence of Eastern European folk music manifests itself in Bartok's use of additive meter, in which beats are organized into combinations of twos and threes. It is also manifest in his use of harmonic clashes of seconds and his use of the octotonic scale, which is very similar to the gypsy scale of North African and Middle Eastern origin. In this lecture, we discuss Bartok's virtuosic Piano Concerto no. 2 of 1931, with its otherworldly "night" music and its homage to Johann Sebastian Bach, and his Concerto for Orchestra of 1943, one of the great orchestral masterworks of the 20th century.

Outline

I. Bela Bartok (1881–1945) composed seven concerti: three for piano, two for violin, one for viola, and a concerto for orchestra. In this lecture, we look at the Piano Concerto no. 2 of 1931 and the Concerto for Orchestra of 1943 as examples of Bartok's compositional style and output.

   A. Bartok's music is *synthetic* in the best sense of the word. **Musical selection:** Bartok, Piano Concerto no. 2, movement 3, opening.

   B. Bartok's music combines:
   1. Melodic and harmonic elements from his native Hungary, as well as Eastern Europe and North Africa.
   2. A rhythmic palette drawn largely from Eastern European folk music, in particular Bulgarian and Thracian music.
   3. An enduring affection for Classical-era forms.
   4. An impeccable German-styled compositional technique; Bartok never wastes a note and everything is packed with meaning.

      5. All this, in addition to Bartok's innate dramatic genius, his skills as a performer (he was one of the great pianists of his generation), and his deep and moral humanity, culminates in a musical synthesis of utterly unlike elements.

  C. For some time after his death in 1945, Bartok's importance as a composer was downgraded by the generation of musical modernists that appeared after World War II. Despite the power and craft of his music, he was seen as an evolutionary dead end, a Romantic nationalist composing in a semi-modern style that had no place in the post-World War II world.

  D. Today, we know better. It is not just the stylistic content of Bartok's music that makes it so important but also the process of synthesis that Bartok's music represents. His music is viscerally exciting and intellectually rewarding, modern without being dogmatic; it sings and it rocks. **Musical selection:** Bartok, Piano Concerto no. 2, movement 3, conclusion.

  E. Bartok's music is personal, powerful, and brilliantly crafted; it manages to reconcile diverse aspects of the global environment into a whole greater than its parts. Bartok is a composer for our time.

II. Because of his various childhood illnesses, Bartok spent a tremendous amount of time at home, listening to his mother play the piano and learning to play the piano himself. By the time he was 11 years old, he was concertizing; by 15, he was working as a professional accompanist, and a year later, he was composing music of genuine interest.

  A. Bartok was a superb pianist, whose recordings are still available. He might have made a career as a pianist, except that, in 1902, he heard a performance of Richard Strauss's *Thus Spake Zarathustra*. The work inspired him to compose.

  B. Between 1902 and 1905, Bartok wrote music that was more influenced by Brahms, Strauss, and his essentially German musical education than anything else.

  C. That began to change in 1905, when he and his friend and fellow composer Zoltan Kodaly began to travel around Eastern Europe recording authentic folk music, which eventually exerted a powerful influence on Bartok's own music.

D. Despite the "modernity" of his music, Bartok was not a revolutionary. He was a synthesist, combining Eastern European folk-music elements with a rigorous Germanic approach to compositional technique and musical form.

E. In terms of rhythm in Bartok's music, his amazing additive meters were inspired by the additive meters of Bulgarian folk music: In Western European music, the "beat" is typically organized in groups of two or three, a type of organization we call *duple* and *triple meter*. In many Eastern European folk traditions, meter consists of some *combination* of twos and threes—something called *additive meter*.

  1. The following excerpt is from a Thracian song (the Rhodope region of southern Bulgaria) entitled "*Devoiko Devoiko Mome*" ("My Girl"). The meter is a five-beat pattern, perceived as a two plus a three: 1 + 2 – 1 + 2 + 3. **Musical selection:** "*Devoiko Devoiko Mome.*"
  2. The third movement of Bartok's String Quartet no. 5 of 1934 is marked *alla Bulgarese* ("as in Bulgaria") —a specific reference to the movement's additive meter of 4 + 2 + 3. **Musical selection:** Bartok, String Quartet no. 5, movement 3, opening. That rhythm is perfectly natural to Bartok.

F. In terms of Bartok's harmonic language, his sense of consonance and dissonance also grew as much from his contact with Eastern European folk music as from his Western European training. This is illustrated by a song called "*Tambura Dranka*" from Bulgaria, where a favorite harmonic effect is obtained through the dissonance caused when one voice comes within a major or minor second of a second voice. **Musical selection:** "*Tambura Dranka.*"

  1. The basic harmonic units in Western tonal music are built by stacking thirds. **Piano example:** C–E–G.
  2. Bartok, however, is just as at home with harmonic units that include major and minor seconds. **Piano example:** C–A and F–C–G–D–A–E.
  3. Bartok perceives such harmonies as perfect consonances. **Musical selection:** Bartok, Piano Concerto no. 2, movement 2, opening.

G. In terms of Bartok's sense of melody, his themes are based on pitch collections of non-Western European origin. For example, the amazing third-movement opening of his Piano Concerto no. 2 is based on a scale called an *octotonic scale*, a construct very close to one of North African and Middle Eastern origin called the *gypsy scale*. **Piano example:** C–D–Eb–F–F#–G#–A–B–C. **Musical selection:** Bartok, Piano Concerto no. 2, movement 3, opening.

H. These are just a few of the musical elements and influences that Bartok absorbed through his study of Eastern European, Turkish, and North African folk music. He synthesized amazingly different musical traditions and, in doing so, created a music that is utterly original and striking.

III. Bartok made his living as a pianist and music teacher. In 1907, he was appointed professor of piano at the Budapest Conservatory, a position that he held for more than 30 years. When he came to the United States in 1940 and was offered a position teaching composition at the Curtis Institute, he explained that he had never wanted to teach composition, because it jeopardized his own composing.

A. Much of Bartok's piano music was written for his own performance, as was his Piano Concerto no. 2 of 1931, which is structured as a large-scale arch, or *palindrome*.

1. The work is cast in three movements, and the third-movement rondo is a mirror image of the first-movement rondo. The first movement's rondo theme becomes the third movement's theme B, and the first movement's theme B becomes the third movement's rondo theme.

2. The second movement is in three-part, A–B–A form. The B section—the capstone of the concerto's large-scale arch design—is a buzzing, squealing, absolutely incredible bit of "night" music. **Musical selection:** Bartok, Piano Concerto no. 2, movement 2, B opening.

3. When it comes to creating otherworldly dreamscapes in middle movements, only Mozart and Debussy are Bartok's equals.

B. The first movement of the Piano Concerto no. 2 is scored for piano, percussion, winds, and brass only. With its relatively spare scoring and its melodic content and form, the movement pays clear homage to Johann Sebastian Bach, in particular, Bach's trumpet-dominated *Brandenburg* Concerto no. 2. It begins with a rising piano scale that introduces a bright, blaring fanfare, immediately establishing a propulsive, celebratory mood. **Musical selection:** Bartok, Piano Concerto no. 2, movement 1, opening fanfare (played twice).

C. Across the span of both the first and third movements, this fanfare will be used as a ritornello. In this first movement, we hear it seven times in some form or another, as it punctuates each appearance of the rondo theme and introduces the cadenza. For example, the second appearance of the ritornello fanfare appears immediately after the rondo theme and before the first contrasting episode. **Musical selection:** Bartok, Piano Concerto no. 2, movement 1, ritornello 2.

   1. The third appearance of the ritornello fanfare follows the first restatement of the rondo theme. **Musical selection:** Bartok, Piano Concerto no. 2, movement 1, ritornello 3.

   2. The fourth appearance of the ritornello fanfare follows the second restatement of the rondo theme, and so forth.

   3. The rondo theme itself has the sort of chattering melody, motoric rhythms, and harmonic underpinning that we associate with the melodies of the Baroque era. **Musical selections:** Bartok, Piano Concerto no. 2, movement 1, rondo theme, compared with Bach, *Brandenburg* Concerto no. 2 in F Major, BWV 1047, movement 1, ritornello theme.

   4. Bartok's reference to Bach in the first movement of his concerto becomes explicit during the third contrasting episode, or the D section of this rondo, when the piano and orchestra suddenly play a wonderful little take-off on a Bach invention. **Musical selection:** Bartok, Piano Concerto no. 2, movement 1, D, Bach quote.

   5. Like Prokofiev, Bartok conceived of the piano as being as much a percussion instrument as a stringed instrument, and throughout the concerto, he teams the piano with various percussion instruments to great effect. For example, the first-movement cadenza is initiated by the timpani, which gently strokes the piano into action. **Musical selection:** Bartok, Piano Concerto no. 2, movement 1, fanfare, ritornello 6, and cadenza.

D. Let us once again sample the rock 'n roll inferno that is the third-movement rondo theme, noting that the movement is initiated by the bass drum and that the rondo theme itself is accompanied by both bass drum and timpani. **Musical selection:** Bartok, Piano Concerto no. 2, movement 3, rondo theme.

1. As in the first movement, the cadenza in this third movement is aided and abetted by the drums, in this case a brutal, pounding bass drum. Let us hear what is, including the first movement, the ninth version of the ritornello fanfare, which initiates this third-movement cadenza. This is followed by the "wailin' and stompin'" cadenza, then a swirling, disembodied passage that refers back to the second movement, followed by the tenth and final appearance of the ritornello fanfare and the conclusion of the movement. **Musical selection:** Bartok, Piano Concerto no. 2, movement 3, conclusion.

2. In the words of Professor Michael Thomas Roeder:

   > In this concerto, Bartok succeeds in synthesizing the musical styles that so interested him. It incorporates the motivic and thematic development of Beethoven, the contrapuntal artistry of Bach, the impressionistic techniques of Debussy, the thematic transformation and pianistic virtuosity of Liszt, and the scale structures and rhythmic features of [Eastern European] folk music. All are combined with a logical organization of the highest artistic merit to form a work of sensuous beauty and dynamic power. (Roeder, p. 384.)

IV. Adolf Hitler came to power in 1933. Repulsed by the rise of Nazism and knowing it was only a matter of time before Hungary would be occupied by the Nazis, Bartok immigrated to the United States early in 1940. The following year, he was diagnosed with leukemia and was hospitalized in 1943.

   A. In June of 1943, Sergei Koussevitzky, conductor of the Boston Symphony Orchestra, visited Bartok in the hospital and offered him a major commission to compose what would become the Concerto for Orchestra. Bartok's depression lifted and his appetite returned.

   B. During periods of remission, Bartok worked on the concerto, composing most of it in seven weeks! It is one of the great orchestral masterworks of the 20th century and remains Bartok's most frequently performed orchestral work.

C. The piece is set in five movements, and Bartok called it a concerto, not a symphony, because of the virtuosic orchestral and solo writing that permeates the score: Every principal player and many section players, as well, have featured solos. The work received its premiere in Boston on December 1, 1944.

D. Bartok wrote in his program note: "The general mood of the work represents, apart from the jesting second movement, a gradual transition from the sternness of the first movement and the lugubrious death-song of the third, to the life-assertion of the fifth." **Musical selection:** Bartok, Concerto for Orchestra, movement 5, opening.

E. Bartok never saw his beloved Hungary again. His New York apartment, just a few blocks from Carnegie Hall, was where he lived in "comfortable exile." He died in New York's West Side Hospital on September 26, 1945.

Lecture Twenty-One
Schönberg, Berg and the 12-Tone Method

Scope: Arnold Schönberg was one of the most influential composers of the 20th century. Believing in melody and polyphony as the essence of music, he created compositions in which he "emancipated" melody from—as he saw it—the arbitrary rules of consonance and dissonance. These freely atonal works, written between 1908 and 1913, had enormous impact on Western music. By 1925, Schönberg developed a musical system that answered his need to convey a sense of departure and return in his music; it would be his counterpart to the traditional harmonic fundamentals of tension and resolution. Known as the 12-tone method, Schönberg's system uses all 12 pitches of the chromatic scale as a matrix of tone rows or sets of pitches that can be organized, rearranged, and motivically exploited to create a complete composition. In deploying his rows, Schönberg arrives at transparent chordal textures, polyphony that can be as complex as Johann Sebastian Bach's, and lush melodic accompaniments that are housed in traditional formal structures. As an example of his 12-tone music, we look at the viscerally powerful Piano Concerto, op. 42, of 1942. We also look at the haunting Violin Concerto of Schönberg's student Alban Berg, whose use of the 12-tone technique in this work is stunningly expressive and lyric.

Outline

I. **Musical selection:** Schönberg, Piano Concerto, op. 42 (1942), movement 1, theme 1. There has never been a more talented, important, misunderstood, and underappreciated composer than Arnold Schönberg (1874–1951).

   A. Schönberg himself insisted that he was a traditionalist, that his music had developed "from the traditions of German music," and that his "teachers" had "primarily" been Bach and Mozart and "secondarily, Beethoven, Brahms and Wagner."

   B. He believed that his music was the next logical step in the evolution of German/Austrian music. He believed in great craft, motivic development, Baroque and Classical-era forms, and the

German predilection for seriousness and profundity in music. He particularly believed in melody as the essential element in music and in polyphony (the art of combining and balancing multiple simultaneous melodies).

C. Increasingly, what he did not believe in was the tonal harmonic system of consonance and dissonance, tension and resolution, major/minor chords, and so forth. He came to view the tonal system, operative in Western music since the 1400s, as an impingement on melody, limiting it by forcing melodies to adhere to what he believed were artificial constructs: harmonies. He wanted melody to be allowed to develop unhindered by the "underbrush" of harmony.

D. Between 1908 and 1913, Schönberg experimented with suspending the rules of traditional tonal harmony in favor of music in which melody, polyphony, and motivic transformation were the be-alls and end-alls. He referred to this period as the "emancipation of dissonance."

E. By studiously avoiding traditional tonal constructs, Schönberg created a music ruled not by what he considered the arbitrary rules of consonance and dissonance but of pure melodic development and transformation. He saw himself as a simplifier. The freely atonal works that he composed between 1908 and 1913 include the *Five Pieces for Orchestra*, *Erwartung*, and *Pierrot Lunaire*. These works changed the course of Western music.

F. Schönberg realized how difficult his music sounded to audiences, but he was convinced that he had a mission to take music to the next step. He called himself a "conservative who was forced to become a radical."

II. Schönberg was born in a poor, Orthodox Jewish household. He began playing violin at eight years old and composing soon thereafter. He was almost entirely self-taught as a composer, and his first major works, *Transfigured Night* (1899), *Pelleas and Melisande* (1903), and the String Quartet no. 1 (1905), are fully within the late-19th-century German Romantic tradition of Wagner, Mahler, and Richard Strauss. It was a tradition rooted in harmonic language that, in the words of the pianist Glenn Gould, "became more complicated [as it grew older]…all that was left to add to this language was the deliberate slackening of discipline, the willingness, in fact, to do for an expressive reason the wrong thing" (Gould, p. 5).

A. Schönberg came of age in an increasingly anti-Semitic Austrian Empire, and his alienation from his home culture manifested itself, among other ways, in a particularly intense mode of musical expression, which ultimately broke with traditional tonality, thereby opening a door to an entirely new world of musical expression.

B. In 1923, Schönberg was at a crossroad. He realized that if he wanted to compose large-scale works, he needed some way of creating a sense of departure and return, an analog to the tonal system's elements of tension and resolution.

    1. Over the next two years, he formulated an entirely new way of organizing pitch that he called his "method of composing with twelve tones which are related only with one another."

    2. A *12-tone composition* is based on something called a *12-tone row*, an ordering of all 12 chromatic pitches, arranged in such a way that no one pitch is emphasized before the others have all been heard. The 12-tone row is no more a theme than the key of C major is a theme. It is just a series of pitches and pitch relationships that can be mined and manipulated to create a piece of music.

C. The 12-tone row may be used in any one of four different forms:

    1. In its original, or prime form.

    2. In inversion (upside down).

    3. In retrograde (backwards).

    4. In retrograde inversion (backwards and upside down).

    5. Each one of these row forms can be transposed to begin on any 1 of the 12 pitches of the chromatic scale, which means that a single 12-tone row has 48 permutations: 12 prime sets, 12 inversions, 12 retrogrades, and 12 retrograde inversions.

    6. It is from this matrix of 48 different rows, or sets of pitches, that a composer creates melodies, polyphony, and harmonies. Rhythms, phrases, musical textures, musical form—all of these are determined by the ear and imagination of the composer—all the 12-tone method does is supply a series of pitches and pitch relationships that "color" a given work in the same way that major and minor scales "color" the sound of a tonal composition.

D. Each 12-tone composition creates its own pitch environment, unique and knowable only to that particular piece, although it is still up to the composer to determine how to deploy a 12-tone row, and in this, Schönberg was a complete traditionalist:
  1. He created long, lush melodies with gorgeous accompaniments.
  2. He created undulating and transparent chordal textures, as well as dense, Bach-like thickets of polyphony.
  3. His phrase structures and musical forms hearken back to the Classical and even the Baroque eras.

E. One last key point: Schönberg insisted that his music be judged as such and not as the manifestation of a system.

III. Schönberg composed two concerti: the Violin Concerto, op. 36, completed in 1936, and the Piano Concerto, op. 42, of 1942.

A. In his book *Fundamentals of Musical Composition*, Schönberg advocates that a composition should be written with a stimulus (such as a poem, story, play, or movie) in mind. The stimulus for his Piano Concerto was a poem that referred to World War II, which was in its darkest days when Schönberg wrote the concerto in 1942:

> Life was so easy
> [When] suddenly hatred broke out;
> A grave situation was created,
> But life goes on. (Whittal)

B. "Life was so easy": The first movement of the concerto (*andante*) begins quietly and gently, with the solo piano presenting a graceful, waltzing theme 1. **Musical selection:** Schönberg, Piano Concerto, op. 42, movement 1, theme 1.
  1. After a brief transition (which cannot be called a modulating bridge, because this is not tonal music), we arrive at theme 2, a wistful, delicate theme that features a solo clarinet and oboe. Following the theme, the violins take the lead: They play a long, sustained melody over a busy accompaniment provided by the piano, which brings the exposition to its conclusion.

Musical selection: Schönberg, Piano Concerto, op. 42, movement 1, theme 2 and exposition conclusion.

   2. The formal structure here is as clear as can be. Schönberg's melodic phrases rise and fall just as in tonal music; the dialogue and textures we hear between the piano and the orchestra are the same sorts we would hear in traditional tonal music; the sense of foreground, middle ground, and background we perceive are the same as we would hear in traditional tonal music. Moreover, in order to clearly articulate the sonata form, Schönberg pauses before moving from one large section to the next. Frankly, this music hardly sounds "modern" at all.

   3. As the movement moves through the development section and recapitulation, a sense of dramatic urgency grows: Phrases become shorter and choppier, the activity level increases, and the music gets louder—Schönberg is building toward the dark emotional world of the second movement, which begins without a pause.

C. "Suddenly hatred broke out": A typical three-part, A–B–A scherzo features fast, violent, fragmented outer sections and a somewhat slower, more tranquil B section. While we listen to the opening A section, let us be especially alert to Schönberg's use of the xylophone, which gives explosive point to this music, and the snare drum, which creates the martial effect that evokes "the war." **Musical selection:** Schönberg, Piano Concerto, op. 42, movement 2, opening.

D. "A grave situation was created": The slow third movement (*adagio*), consisting of a theme and five variations, is the expressive center of the concerto. The theme itself, a melody of great emotional depth and sadness, is presented without the piano, by strings, bassoon, and oboe. **Musical selection:** Schönberg, Piano Concerto, op. 42, movement 3, theme.

   1. The movement builds to a tremendous climax: a forlorn and finally violent funeral march that constitutes the fifth and final variation. **Musical selection:** Schönberg, Piano Concerto, op. 42, movement 3, variation 5.

   2. A brief cadenza for piano follows that puts some distance between the devastating conclusion of the third movement and the comparatively upbeat fourth and final movement.

- **E.** "But life goes on": Marked *giocoso* ("playfully"), the fourth movement is a garden-variety rondo, structured as A–B–A–C–A. **Musical selection:** Schönberg, Piano Concerto, op. 42, movement 4, rondo theme.
- **F.** The coda brings forth some real pianistic fireworks, and the movement concludes with a C major chord! **Musical selection:** Schönberg, Piano Concerto, op. 42, movement 4, coda.
- **G.** Schönberg's music—all of it—is viscerally powerful, dauntingly complex, often extremely difficult to play, and yet, hauntingly beautiful.

IV. Schönberg's 12-tone technique was teachable and exportable from one student to another. It could be used by any composer and adapted to his or her particular sensibilities or needs. The same cannot be said of Schönberg's contemporaries, Debussy and Stravinsky. If one employs the compositional techniques pioneered by those composers, the result is music that sounds like the music of those composers. One of the reasons that Schönberg was an important teacher was because he was able to help his students discover their own musical voices.

- **A.** Among those students was Alban Berg (1885–1935), who, along with Anton Webern, was Schönberg's most important student and disciple.
- **B.** A modest inheritance, augmented by the success of his opera *Wozzeck*, allowed Berg the freedom to compose slowly and meticulously. Among his smallish output are two of the great operas in the repertoire, *Wozzeck* (1914–1922) and *Lulu*, begun in 1929 and left unfinished at his death in 1935.
- **C.** Two events gave birth to Berg's Violin Concerto.
    1. The Russian-born American violinist Louis Krasner was so impressed by *Wozzeck* that he offered Berg a commission to compose a violin concerto. When Berg hesitated, Krasner suggested that only Berg could compose a 12-tone concerto lyric and expressive enough to destroy the stereotype of 12-tone music as being "all brain and no heart" (Steinberg, p. 97).
    2. On April 22, 1935, Manon Gropius, daughter of Alma Mahler and her second husband, the famed Bauhaus architect Walter Gropius, died. Berg adored Manon and was crushed by her death. His Violin Concerto became his requiem for her. He

dedicated the score to Louis Krasner and "to the memory of an angel."
- **D.** Berg was even more of a Romantic throwback than Schönberg.
    1. The 12-tone row that Schönberg used to build his Piano Concerto was purposely designed not to suggest any particular key area and not to suggest anything that might sound like a traditional chord. **Piano example:** Schönberg's row.
    2. As Schönberg arrays this row across the span of his concerto, its essential atonality guarantees that the music built from it will be, likewise, atonal in nature.
    3. But if we build a row using more "consonant" intervals, ones that at least imply the sound of traditional harmonies, we might get a 12-tone row that sounds like this. **Piano example:** Greenberg's row.
    4. It is possible, then, to compose a strictly 12-tone piece that nevertheless implies tonality and traditional harmonies without actually deploying them. **Piano example:** Greenberg, *Song of the Spheres*, measure 1–downbeat 16.
    5. Berg employs the following vaguely tonal sounding row in his Violin Concerto. It consists of a series of interlocking thirds, the interval used to build traditional tonal harmonies. The result is a 12-tone row that appears to consist of a series of overlapping major and minor chords, a row that seems to move through an entire series of different "key" areas. **Piano example:** Berg's row.
- **E.** Berg's Violin Concerto (1935) is cast in four movements that are paired to form two large parts. Part 1 (movements 1 and 2) is meant to portray the life of Manon Gropius; part 2 (movements 3 and 4) portray her suffering and death.
    1. The first movement is a three-part, A–B–A form (*andante*). The opening A section consists of an introduction, during which the 12-tone row is spelled out in a series of rising and falling arpeggios. Then follows theme A, during which the rising and falling arpeggios, heard in the solo violin, take on a genuinely thematic quality over a pensive orchestral accompaniment. **Musical selection:** Berg, Violin Concerto, movement 1, A.

    2. This nostalgic, intensely lyric music gives way to a dramatic, rhapsodic contrasting episode that is the B section, followed by a return to the opening music.

F. The second movement follows without a break. It is a scherzo featuring two waltz-like themes that, through some extraordinary alchemy, Berg manages to coax out of his 12-tone row. The first of these most Viennese-y waltzes is heard initially in the clarinets. **Musical selection:** Berg, Violin Concerto, movement 2, waltz no. 1.
    1. The second waltz theme is played by the solo violin. **Musical selection:** Berg, Violin Concerto, movement 2, waltz no. 2.
    2. The music conveys a mood of subtle nostalgia, and the profound grief that lies just below the surface of this music rises to the surface for the briefest of moments during the middle of this second movement.
    3. A most extraordinary event ends the movement: An achingly lyric Carinthian folk tune heard in the horns is heard under a violin countermelody and orchestral accompaniment derived from the 12-tone row. The waltz music suddenly resumes, and then, as if too overcome with dark memories to continue, the music just stops. **Musical selection:** Berg, Violin Concerto, movement 2, conclusion.

G. The violent, grieving third movement, the most outwardly atonal movement of the concerto, speaks explicitly to the pain and rage that were only implied during the second movement.

H. The fourth and final movement is about resignation in the face of the inevitable.
    1. Berg begins it with a Bach chorale entitled, "It Is Enough, Lord, So Take My Soul." The chorale theme is stated initially in the solo violin, which then alternates with very organ-like winds. **Musical selection:** Berg, Violin Concerto, movement 4, chorale.
    2. A tone of quiet pain and dream-like mystery pervades the remainder of the concerto, which concludes with a last heartbreaking statement of the Carinthian folk tune; a heavenly ascent in the solo violin, winds, and strings; and one last rising and falling arpeggio that ends the concerto as it began. **Musical selection:** Berg, Violin Concerto, movement 4, conclusion.

I. The power and beauty of this concerto are off any scale we use or standard we set, even though, aside from the Carinthian folk song and the Bach chorale, it is an entirely 12-tone work.

Lecture Twenty-Two
Twentieth-Century Masters

Scope: In this lecture, we look at five composers and five concerto masterworks. The impassioned Violin Concerto in D Minor, op. 47, by the Finnish composer Jean Sibelius, is all about the Romantic notion of virtuoso as hero. Carl Nielson's Clarinet Concerto, op. 57, of 1928 is an extraordinary work that demonstrates Nielson's fascination with what he called the "dramatic scenario," pitting soloist against orchestra in a tour-de-force of highly theatrical instrumental dialogue. The music of William Walton has a spectacular sense of rhythmic snap that is readily apparent in his Viola Concerto, as is his brilliantly sensitive balance of solo viola and orchestra. With Aaron Copland we come to the single most influential and representative American-born composer of the 20th century. His Piano Concerto of 1926 affords an insight into how jazz was being introduced in the concert hall in the 1920s. Alberto Ginastera's Piano Concerto no. 1 is an attention-grabber, with its tour-de-force of virtuosic, muscular pianism; explosive kinetic power; and sense of mystery. We conclude this lecture with a brief but wholehearted recommendation of other concerti by Samuel Barber, Paul Hindemith, William Schuman, and Igor Stravinsky.

Outline

I. The Finnish composer Jean (Johan) Sibelius (1865–1957) used the language of 19th-century musical Romanticism throughout his compositional life, despite the fact that he lived more than halfway through the 20th century. He simplified the solo part of his highly virtuosic Violin Concerto in D Minor after its premiere in 1903, and it is this revised version of 1905 that we will hear in this lecture.

   A. The concerto is cast in the standard three movements: the first in sonata form, followed by an *adagio* second movement, and an upbeat *allegro* third movement. It opens with one of Sibelius's most inspired passages: Quietly murmuring strings provide a shimmering harmonic background, over which the violin plays an expansive, achingly beautiful theme 1. **Musical selection:**

Sibelius, Violin Concerto in D Minor, op. 47, movement 1, theme 1.

- **B.** It is evident from the outset that this concerto is about the Romantic notion of virtuoso as hero. Despite the fact that there is some outstanding orchestral writing in this work, only rarely will the soloist and orchestra engage in dialogue as equals.
- **C.** The development section is, in its entirety, an impassioned cadenza for the solo violin, punctuated, recitative-like, by a single orchestral exclamation. **Musical selection:** Sibelius, Violin Concerto in D Minor, op. 47, movement 1, development-section cadenza, opening.
- **D.** As will be the case with all the works discussed in this lecture, Sibelius's violin concerto is a masterwork that deserves infinitely more time than we have to give it.

II. The central figure in Danish music in the late 19th and early 20th centuries is Carl Nielsen (1865–1931). Although he was most proficient as a violinist, he retained a special sensitivity for woodwind instruments. His Woodwind Quintet of 1922 is, in my opinion, far and away the best wind quintet in the repertoire, and of his three concerti, two are for wind instruments: a flute concerto (1926) and a clarinet concerto (1928). His violin concerto is a relatively early work, composed in 1911.

- **A.** Nielsen's music has a distinct sound. He was a Classicist in his love of clear melody and expressive directness—Bach, Haydn, and Mozart were his essential models—but his mature music exhibits a quirkiness of harmonic usage and instrumentation and an originality of dramatic interaction that place it firmly within the post-Romantic idiom of the early 20th century.
- **B.** Nielsen's Clarinet Concerto, op. 57, of 1928 was his last major orchestral work, and it demonstrates (as does his Flute Concerto) his late-career fascination with what he referred to as "dramatic scenario": conversation and confrontation between soloists and orchestra.
- **C.** He wrote this work for a friend of his, the clarinetist Aage Oxenvad, whose difficult personality found its way into the concerto, filled as it is with confrontation and argument and only occasional moments of gentleness and calm.

1. The concerto is cast as a single continuous movement, although it is divided into three distinct parts that follow a large-scale fast–slow–fast scheme. We will focus on part 1.
2. The concerto begins, innocently enough, with a quiet if quirky theme 1, played by the 'cellos and basses. **Musical selection:** Nielsen, Clarinet Concerto, op. 57, movement 1, theme 1, opening.
3. Any pretensions to "innocent quietude" disappear soon after the clarinet enters. It plays the opening of the theme, then embarks on a couple of lengthy riffs. The effect is that of a four-year-old on a sugar high mauling a stuffed toy. The orchestra is not amused, and it attempts to get things back on track by insistently playing the theme. **Musical selection:** Nielsen, Clarinet Concerto, op. 57, movement 1, theme 1, clarinet entrance.
4. The relationship between the orchestra and the clarinet goes from bad to worse. The clarinet manages to get a word in edgewise—a little rocking four-note motive—which the orchestra immediately repeats and extends in a mocking tone, as if to say, "You've been a naughty little clarinet not playing the theme as you should!" After about 10 seconds of that orchestral attitude, the clarinet has had enough, and a downright nasty argument between the clarinet and the orchestra follows. **Musical selection:** Nielsen, Clarinet Concerto, op. 57, movement 1, "bad words!"
5. Entirely exasperated, the low strings attempt to play theme 1, only to have the clarinet scream at the top of its register before playing a long melodic idea that has nothing to do with the theme! **Musical selection:** Nielsen, Clarinet Concerto, op. 57, movement 1, theme 1, redux.
6. The orchestra calls for reinforcement, and the snare drum enters. Like the military-styled disciplinarian it represents, it takes on the clarinet in a vain attempt to control and constrain it. The orchestra reenters, and finally, something resembling a truce follows, as both orchestra and clarinet grow quiet in anticipation of theme 2. **Musical selection:** Nielsen, Clarinet Concerto, op. 57, movement 1, snare drum entrance.
7. Nielsen's Clarinet Concerto is about the sometimes collaborative but mostly confrontational relationship between

the clarinet and the orchestra. This is what Nielsen referred to as a "dramatic scenario." It is a tour-de-force of instrumental dialogue, best listened to while imagining three characters standing on stage, one representing the harried, frustrated orchestra; one in military garb, representing the snare drum; and one representing the curmudgeon himself, the clarinetist Aage Oxenvad—all of them attempting to coexist and not doing a very good job at it.

III. Although the compositional style of William Walton (1902–1983) is essentially tonal, his music is filled with melodic and harmonic elements drawn from jazz, rhythmic devices drawn from Stravinsky, and a degree of chromaticism that clearly mark it as belonging to the 20th century. Walton has a spectacular sense of pulse and phrase that makes his music sound as if he had been born in New Orleans, rather than Oldham, England. **Musical selection:** Walton, Viola Concerto, movement 2, opening. In this work, the viola is a full-blooded, deep-throated instrument of great power.

    A. Walton composed three concerti and had the enviable opportunity to write them for three of the greatest performers of the 20th century: The Viola Concerto of 1929, extensively revised in 1962, was composed for Lionel Tertis; the Violin Concerto of 1939 was composed for Jascha Heifetz; and the 'Cello Concerto of 1956 was composed for Gregor Piatigorsky.

    B. Although set in three movements, Walton's Viola Concerto does not follow the time-honored scheme of fast–slow–fast with which we have become so familiar. The first-movement sonata form (*andante*) is the slowish movement; the second-movement scherzo is as fast as a hummingbird's heartbeat; and the third-movement finale is moderately fast.

        1. Movement 1 opens with a brief introductory passage for rising, muted strings that sets the stage for a spacious, resonant, and vaguely bluesy theme, suited perfectly to the viola. **Musical selection:** Walton, Viola Concerto, movement 1, opening.

        2. Movement 3 opens with an introductory, moderately slow solo bassoon passage. After about two minutes, the movement finally explodes into action. Let us join the movement at that point and note how brilliantly Walton balances the viola

against the orchestra by instantly thinning the orchestration when the viola is playing and by making sure that no orchestral instruments compete with the viola in the register in which it's playing. **Musical selection:** Walton, Viola Concerto, movement 3 (*allegro*).
   3. Sometime during the 1930s, the elderly Guido Adler, musicologist, scholar, and close friend of Gustav Mahler, heard Walton's Viola Concerto and greeted it as "the real thing at last!"

IV. Aaron Copland (1900–1990) is the most influential and representative American-born composer of the 20th century. He composed two concerti: one for piano in 1926 and one for clarinet that was commissioned by Benny Goodman in 1948. They are both superb works and are built along the same lines: Each consists of two continuous movements, a slow, lyric first movement, followed by a fast second movement. We will focus on the Piano Concerto because of the jazz elements it contains and for the insight it affords us into the issues surrounding "jazz in the concert hall" during the 1920s.
   A. Copland was influenced equally by the classics he studied in his piano lessons and by the rich, genuinely global musical environment that was, and is, any New Yorker's heritage.
      1. He studied composition and music theory with Nadia Boulanger just outside Paris between 1920 and 1924, during which time he was powerfully influenced by the music of Stravinsky, Ravel, and *Les Six*. He returned to the United States in 1924, just after George Gershwin's *Rhapsody in Blue* was premiered, a piece that went a long way toward "legitimizing" jazz as a serious American music.
      2. Copland was determined to become an "American" composer, and in 1925, that meant writing music that incorporated elements of jazz.
      3. He was commissioned to write a piano concerto by the conductor Serge Koussevitzky, who was in the process of almost single-handedly putting American music on the international map. With Copland at the piano, Koussevitzky conducted the concerto's premiere in Boston on January 28, 1927. The work met with a hostile reception, but public opinion changed over time, and when Leonard Bernstein

reintroduced the work in 1946, it was hailed as "the best roar from the roaring twenties."

B. Copland's Piano Concerto is set in two continuous movements. Copland himself described its jazz elements as "the two basic jazz moods: the slow blues and the snappy number."

C. The concerto begins with an orchestral introduction that features exactly the sort of wide-open melodic intervals that give Copland's music its trademark sense of spaciousness. **Musical selection:** Copland, Piano Concerto, movement 1, introduction.

1. The piano now enters and plays an incredibly spare abstraction of the bluesy melody that will only coalesce when the orchestra reenters about a minute later. In his spareness, Copland is the anti-Liszt; every note counts, and nothing is done for virtuosic effect. We listen to the blues theme as it unfolds. **Musical selection:** Copland, Piano Concerto, movement 1, blues theme.
2. Slowly, the movement builds to a magnificent climax, which is followed by a series of exquisite solos in the winds (including solos for alto and soprano saxophones) that dissipate the energy and pave the way for the second movement. **Musical selection:** Copland, Piano Concerto, movement 1, conclusion.

D. The second movement (the "snappy number") begins with a lengthy cadenza, a sort of Cubist version of the ragtime-derived, stride piano style that was so popular in the 1920s. **Musical selection:** Copland, Piano Concerto, movement 2, cadenza and orchestral entry.

1. About two-thirds of the way through this second movement, the lyric, blues-derived music of the first movement returns for a curtain call, which gives way to an explosive coda and the conclusion of the concerto. **Musical selection:** Copland, Piano Concerto, movement 2, conclusion.
2. This music is angular and brittle, a superb abstraction of the rhythmic elements of jazz as Copland understood jazz at the time.
3. After the concerto's premiere, Copland announced that he was through using jazz in his music, because he felt he had "done all [he] could with the [jazz] idiom." Despite what he said,

however, the jazz idiom, implicitly and often explicitly, continued to inform his music for the rest of his life.

V. Alberto Ginastera (1916–1983), who incidentally, studied with Copland at Tanglewood in 1947, was an avowed music nationalist until the late 1950s. His essential influences, along with the music of his native Argentina, were Stravinsky, Bartok, and Manuel de Falla. Starting around 1958, he began moving away from the explicit folk references that had characterized his music to that point and began experimenting with 12-tone technique and various other modernist methodologies. Having said that, Ginastera's late music, which includes two piano concerti and concerti for harp, violin, and 'cello, is filled with the same visceral rhythmic energy, melodic invention, developmental craft, and expressive joy and mystery as his earlier, less experimental music.

    A. Ginastera's Piano Concerto no. 1 of 1961 was commissioned by the Koussevitzky Foundation at the Library of Congress. Its four movements are a virtual catalog of concerto techniques, as well as Ginastera's own compositional influences and priorities.

    B. The first movement, entitled "Cadenza and Variations," is an explosive, Liszt-inspired, piano-soloist-as-hero tour-de-force of virtuosity and violent confrontations between the piano and the orchestra. In terms of pure, muscular musical bulk, you cannot get much further away from Copland than this. **Musical selection:** Ginastera, Piano Concerto no. 1, op. 28, movement 1, opening.

    C. The surreal second movement, entitled *Scherzo allucinante* (literally, "Hallucinogenic Scherzo"), evokes the magic that is such a strong element in Argentine folk culture.

    D. The third movement (*adagissimo*) is a lyric three-part movement that rises to a tremendous climax in the middle section.

    E. Then, there is the amazing, furious, drum-dominated, piano-as-percussion-instrument, Bartok-gone-mad fourth-movement rondo that we are compelled to sample. Entitled *Toccata concertata* ("Concerto toccata"), it is based on a characteristic Argentine dance rhythm of alternating 6/8 meter with 3/4. **Musical selection:** Ginastera, Piano Concerto no. 1, op. 28, movement 4, opening.

VI. Other composers whose first-class concerti we have not had time to discuss here but that richly deserve attention include:

A. Samuel Barber (1910–1981), who composed three concerti, one for violin, one for 'cello, and a big, lyric, Romantic-styled piano concerto of great power and beauty.

B. Paul Hindemith (1895–1963), a musical polymath, who composed 12 concerti, including a commendable Violin Concerto of 1939 and Horn Concerto of 1949.

C. William Schuman (1910–1992), who wrote a violin concerto and a piano concerto (1942) that is a perfect example of his propulsive, Big-Apple-jazz-influenced style; it is dynamite.

D. Igor Stravinsky (1882–1971), whose Piano Concerto, Violin Concerto, and Concerto in Eb for Chamber Orchestra (known as the *Dumbarton Oaks* Concerto) are among the great masterworks of the 20th century. (These concerti are discussed at length in Professor Greenberg's Teaching Company course *Great Masters: Stravinsky—His Life and Music*.)

Lecture Twenty-Three
Elliott Carter

Scope: Elliott Carter's music enjoys a rich variety of influences, including, among others, the jazzy, creative "roaring 20s" environment in which he grew up; the groundbreaking concerts of Serge Koussevitzky and the Boston Symphony Orchestra; his studies of counterpoint; and such composers as Igor Stravinsky, Charles Ives, and Conlon Nancarrow, whose polyphony was not just that of multiple simultaneous melodies but of multiple simultaneous sorts of music. Carter's great achievement in his mature music is his ability to meld completely different, simultaneous musical elements into a convincing and homogeneous whole. His concerti bring out his proclivity for dramatic contrast, contest, and reconciliation. This is particularly explicit in his Double Concerto for Harpsichord and Piano of 1961, which is also his greatest orchestral work. The dramatic quality of this incredibly complex work must be seen and heard live to be fully appreciated. Spiritually, Carter's mature music represents the democratic ideal that celebrates the uniqueness of the individual voice and recognizes its responsibility to contribute to something greater than itself.

Outline

I. In this lecture, we celebrate one of the most important and admittedly "difficult" composers of the 20th century—Elliott Carter.
   A. We have three goals for this lecture:
      1. To create a musical and historical context for Elliott Carter's mature compositional style and, in doing so, to understand how and why Carter went from writing such music as his *Holiday* Overture of 1944 to his Double Concerto for Harpsichord and Piano of 1961. **Musical selections:** Carter, *Holiday* Overture, opening; Double Concerto for Harpsichord and Piano, movement 3, opening.
      2. To observe the post-World War II modernist musical environment as one in which many composers chose to follow dogma rather than their ears and to understand how Elliott

Carter's music is, at once, extremely "modern" yet entirely free of dogma: inspired, idiosyncratic music like no other.
3. To understand why Carter is, perhaps, the most singularly American composer of the 20th century and why his music is such a perfect metaphor for the democratic ideal.

B. Carter was born in New York City in 1908 and, at the time of this recording, is still going strong.
1. In addition to an excellent education, Carter had the good fortune to grow up in New York during the energetic and creative "roaring 20s." He also had the opportunity to meet and discuss new music with the American composer Charles Ives and to hear Koussevitzky's groundbreaking concerts at Carnegie Hall. In 1925, while in Vienna, he bought every available score by Schönberg, Berg, and Webern. Vacations were spent attending the great European music festivals at Salzburg, Munich, and Bayreuth.
2. He finished his music education, like so many American composers of his generation, by taking lessons with Nadia Boulanger, who lived near Paris and with whom Carter studied the strict counterpoint that would strongly influence his future compositional career.

C. When he returned to the United States in 1935, he entered a cultural environment in which the emphasis was on musical populism—the artistic spirit of the time was to create music that was accessible to the entire American community, music that used the familiar harmonic and melodic structures of traditional tonality and, somehow, evoked "America" in sound or in spirit.
1. The "neo-tonal" American music written between the mid-1930s and mid-1940s included jazz elements (such as Gershwin's *Porgy and Bess*), folk influences (such as Copland's *Billy the Kid*), and patriotic elements, particularly in the music written during World War II.
2. The music that Carter wrote between his return to the United States in 1935 and the end of World War II in 1945 fits into this category. His *Holiday* Overture (1944) opens with explosive and joyful music, inspired by the liberation of Paris. **Musical selection:** Carter, *Holiday* Overture, opening.
3. At that time, Carter, like most American composers, believed that art music had a duty to be accessible to the "American

public," its language purposefully breaking from the chromatic, emotionally stormy music of German Expressionism, which Carter saw as "part of the madness that led to Hitler" (although, by his own admission, it continued to inspire him as a source of ideas).

II. In the years following World War II, attitudes changed toward the nature of musical expression. The rise of Hitler and fascism was perceived as a function of mystical Romanticism, intensified by a virulent brand of "exclusionary nationalism." As a result, many of the best young American and European postwar composers turned away from an expressive musical philosophy based primarily on "feeling" and "ear" toward one based primarily on "intellect" and "technique."

   A. Carter's musical development and experimentation was part of a larger cultural shift from Romantic to postwar musical expression. What makes Carter different from most postwar modernists is that he never dogmatically utilized formulaic processes to construct his music; he never abandoned his ear as the final arbiter of what he put on paper.

   1. Carter's music is unerringly dramatic and rhythmically engaging. Difficult though his postwar music may be, he never forgets that his audiences need to hang their ears on something when hearing his works for the first time.
   2. The end of World War II had a liberating effect on Carter's music. He fell back in love with the music of Stravinsky, Schönberg, and Bartok and fell out of love with the idea of trying to write the sort of direct, accessible music that had seemed so important during the war.
   3. At the core of his evolving musical style was polyphony—the art of combining melodies. This became the central, driving principle behind his mature music. When he refers to "simultaneous streams of different things going on together," he means not just the simultaneous presentation of different melodies but of entirely different musics—a sort of grand polyphony, or "mega-counterpoint," which had its origin in the music of three of Carter's favorite composers: Stravinsky, Ives, and Conlon Nancarrow.

   B. In Stravinsky's *The Rite of Spring* (1912), various repeated musical patterns (*ostinati*) are often layered one atop the other.

Musical drama and momentum are created, not by traditional means, such as variation or contrast or key changes, but through the interaction and interface of these simultaneous but different musical parts. For example, in the "Procession of the Sage" episode, four different ostinati are layered on top of each other, creating a passage in which multiple musics are presented simultaneously. **Musical selection:** Stravinsky, *The Rite of Spring*, "Procession of the Sage."

- **C.** At exactly the same time in the United States, Charles Ives was also experimenting with simultaneous presentation of different musics but to very different effect. For example, in the third movement of his *Holiday* Symphony, entitled "The Fourth of July," Ives evokes an entire narrative of simultaneous celebratory activities, from the cannon on the green and the village band on Main Street to fire crackers, a baseball game, a fireworks show that sets the town hall ablaze, and much else. There is so much happening in this music that it often takes two conductors to conduct it. **Musical selection:** Ives, "The Fourth of July" from *Holiday* Symphony (1912).
- **D.** Conlon Nancarrow, who was born in Arkansas in 1912 and died in Mexico City in 1997, studied with Walter Piston, Nicolas Slonimsky, and Roger Sessions. In the 1930s, he worked as a jazz trumpeter and studied Indian and African music with Henry Cowell at the New School in New York City. He dedicated most of his creative life to the composition of a series of some 60 studies for player piano. His experiments with polymusic and polyrhythm fascinated Carter. **Musical selection:** Nancarrow, Study for Player Piano no. 2B.
- **E.** We can see from Stravinsky, Ives, and Nancarrow that the mature music of Carter comes from a concept of polyphony as not just multiple, simultaneous melodies but as multiple, simultaneous sorts of music.

III. Carter's breakthrough piece was his Sonata for 'Cello and Piano, which he completed on his 40th birthday on December 11, 1948. It is a masterwork, astonishing in its breadth, its drama, and its originality.

- **A.** In the first movement, the 'cello and piano square off as adversaries. The issue of their reconciliation is the dramatic basis of the entire piece. In the first movement, the storyline presents the collision of and dialogue between two utterly different musical elements: the mechanical (the piano) against the lyric (the 'cello), which can be seen as a metaphor for the inexorable march of time against human striving. **Musical selection:** Carter, Sonata for 'Cello and Piano, movement 1, opening.

B. The collisions of unlike musical parts that characterize Carter's mature music do not have the accidental quality characteristic of Ives, nor the calculated quality of Stravinsky, but rather, an interactive quality, sometimes conversational, sometimes argumentative—the quality that lies at the heart of concertato style.

C. By 1950, Carter was ready to write a piece of music the likes of which he had not written before—the String Quartet no. 1 of 1951.
  1. This work, set in four continuous movements, quickly found its way into the contemporary repertoire and established Carter's international reputation.
  2. It is in the first movement, entitled "Fantasia," that Carter's experiment with simultaneous contrasting musics (polymusic) is most explicitly spelled out.
  3. The instruments enter one by one: first the 'cello, then the second violin, then the first violin, and last, the viola. Each instrument presents a different theme with a tempo and character of its own. The 'cello presents a dramatic, recitative-like passage; the second violin, an off-kilter, pizzicato theme; the first violin, a soaring, singing, long-breathed line; and the viola, a steady-state melody in quarter-note triplets. **Musical selection:** Carter, String Quartet no. 1, movement 1, opening.
  4. Although the four instruments of the quartet will, on occasion, share their particular musical elements with one another, the dramatic "point" of the movement is clear from the beginning: the exploration of simultaneous contrast and conflict, in which, nevertheless, the whole is still greater than its parts.
  5. What Carter has done here is make concurrent a process that is usually consecutive. Ordinarily, contrasting musical ideas are laid out one after the other so that we perceive them as independent elements, whose differences create conflict that can be explored and, perhaps, even resolved later in the piece. In this first movement, Carter has skipped the entire first part of the structural process—the exposition—and jumped

directly into the development, where thematic materials go head-to-head with each other.

IV. The concerto is a genre perfectly suited to Carter's dramatic compositional proclivities toward contrast and contest. Carter composed four concerti: the Piano Concerto of 1965, the Concerto for Orchestra of 1970, the Oboe Concerto of 1987, and the Double Concerto for Harpsichord and Piano with Two Chamber Orchestras, composed between 1956 and 1961. The Double Concerto is both his greatest orchestral work and the concerto in which his ideas of contrast and reconciliation of separate simultaneous musics is most explicitly realized.

  A. The harpsichord and piano are each accompanied by their own orchestra. The only instrument the two orchestras have in common is the horn.

  B. Carter specifies that the two orchestras be as far apart on the stage as possible, and each orchestra has its own melodic, harmonic, and rhythmic material.

  C. Aside from the grand contrasts inherent between the two soloists and their accompanying orchestras, Carter also exploits contrasts within the orchestras themselves. In terms of contrast, contest, and conflict, Carter's Double Concerto is the ultimate concerto. The miracle is that the whole thing not only hangs together but works as an integrated whole.

  D. This work, which must be heard live and seen to be understood, is cast in seven continuous movements arrayed as an arch. The first-movement introduction and the seventh-movement coda bookend the concerto. The second movement is a cadenza for harpsichord, and the sixth movement features cadenzas for the piano. The third movement (*allegro scherzando*) features the piano and its orchestra with harpsichord interruptions, and the fifth movement features the harpsichord and its orchestra with piano interruptions. The fourth movement (*adagio*) is the longest movement and lies at the center of the arch.

  E. The large-scale dramatic progression of the Double Concerto moves from chaos to order and back to chaos. The fourth movement at the center of the arch represents order, as the two orchestras and soloists play as a single unified ensemble. **Musical**

selection: Carter, Double Concerto for Harpsichord and Piano, movement 4, center.

F. We get a sense of the incredible degree of complexity and independence of musical parts if we listen immediately to the seventh and climactic final section of the concerto, the coda. **Musical selection:** Carter, Double Concerto for Harpsichord and Piano, movement 7, coda.

G. This is not easy listening, but it is brilliant, original, and—in live performances—great theater.

H. Throughout his compositional career, and particularly from the 1950s on, Carter has proven himself to be a quintessentially American composer, not in the folkloric sense but more profoundly. What lies at the heart of Carter's mature music is the democratic ideal, an Enlightenment-inspired vision that recognizes the validity, the genius, the uniqueness of each individual voice, as well as the essential responsibility of that voice to contribute to something greater than itself. The amazing diversity of Carter's musical textures and their interplay is a mirror of American society itself.

Lecture Twenty-Four
Servants to the Cause and Guilty Pleasures

Scope: This lecture is organized into three parts. In the first, we look at how concerti are performed—the relationship among soloist, conductor, and orchestra. In the second part, we focus on some composers and superb concerti that have not been discussed thus far in the course. They are: John Ireland and his over-the-top Romantic Piano Concerto in Eb Major; George Gershwin and his Piano Concerto in F; Joaquin Rodrigo and his *Concierto de Aranjuez*, the most popular guitar concerto ever composed; Donald Erb and his incredibly exciting Trombone Concerto; and John Corigliano and his marvelous Oboe Concerto, one of my favorite 20th-century concerti. Finally, we consider a list of composers "to watch." These are living composers who have composed concerti and who promise to compose more. They have not otherwise been included in the course because their work is impossible to appraise as a whole thus far, but this should not preclude seeking out and exploring their music. They are Christopher Rouse, Aaron Jay Kernis, Ellen Taafe Zwilich, Philip Glass, and Jennifer Higdon.

Outline

I. The performance of a concerto is ripe with potential for interpersonal conflict that goes beyond the usual conductor-versus-orchestra warfare. By adding an outsider—a featured soloist—to the mix, we are witness to an exponential increase in the likelihood for interpersonal rivalry, resentment, envy, and sabotage.

A. The entire concept of a featured visiting soloist is potentially testy, because many members of a world-class orchestra are just as capable of playing the solo part of a concerto as any soloist that orchestral management brings in from the outside.

B. But the public does not pay to see the "regular" orchestral players play concerti. Audiences want "stars" to play concerti, even though the "stars" are sometimes not even as good as the resident players.

C. Thus, the potential for animosity between orchestra members and visiting soloists is tremendous, especially if a soloist is not really good. On top of this, many conductors often have mixed feelings about sharing "their" stages with soloists.

D. The relationship between a conductor and soloist is complex and can vary widely. As explained by Erich Leinsdorf, who at one point in his career directed the Boston Symphony Orchestra, soloists are cleared with the music director and *prominent* guest conductors; other conductors do not have a say about which soloists they will be teamed with. According to Leinsdorf, the superstar pianist Vladimir Horowitz once agreed to play a concerto with the New York Philharmonic, choosing the piece, the hall, the conductor, and the concert date, and he made sure that his personal interpretive ideas prevailed, even to advising the conductor! Then there are conductors who agree to perform with only those soloists who will submit to their dictates.

E. A bad performance is almost always blamed on the soloist, regardless of whether it is his or her fault.
   1. Apart from staying together, the most important and potentially tendentious issue between soloist and conductor is that of tempo: the actual speed of the music. In an ideal world, the conductor would always accede to the wishes of the soloist, but we do not live in an ideal world.
   2. Sometimes the differences between soloist and conductor are so great that a performance must be cancelled.

F. The relationship between the soloist and the composer is quite different. Sometimes, as we saw in the Tchaikovsky lecture, a soloist will refuse to play a concerto composed for him. But much more common are the genuine love stories between soloists and composers, relationships in which a soloist both inspires and helps a composer to create a concerto, as, for example, the relationship between Shostakovich and the 'cellist Rostropovich.

II. Concerti are usually of secondary importance on a concert program. They are typically not allotted much rehearsal time. Interpretive decisions are not usually left to the soloist. The proper orchestral balance with the soloist is often not taken into consideration, and the guest performer is not infrequently made to feel unwelcome.

III. We now turn to some "guilty pleasures" that we have not had an opportunity to discuss until now.

A. The music of the English composer John Ireland (1879–1962) is rooted in the Romantic tradition and powerfully influenced by his own Celtic heritage. His piano concerto of 1930 is the most unabashedly over-the-top high-Romantic concerto this side of Rachmaninoff and, sadly, an unfairly neglected masterwork of 20th-century English music. We hear the martial and extremely virtuosic/heroic introduction for piano and orchestra, which leads to a brilliant and, eventually, blaring rondo theme. **Musical selection:** Ireland, Piano Concerto in Eb Major, movement 3, introduction and rondo theme.

B. George Gershwin (1898–1937) was one of the greatest melodists of all time. In 1923, he was approached by the bandleader Paul Whiteman to compose a "serious" concert work in the "jazz idiom" for piano and jazz band. Gershwin hesitated; he had virtually no compositional training, but he found himself forced into action when a notice appeared in the New York papers announcing that he was composing just such a piece. The result was *Rhapsody in Blue*, which was orchestrated by Whiteman's orchestrator, Ferde Grofe, and premiered, with Gershwin at the piano, at New York's Aeolian Hall on February 12, 1924.

    1. *Rhapsody in Blue* is essentially a medley of great tunes linked by some very bad transitions. Despite its shortcomings, the piece ended up serving a purpose much greater than itself, because in writing it, Gershwin was bitten by the concert-composing bug at exactly the time when the American artistic community was coming to believe that jazz was "America's classical music."

    2. Technically, Gershwin's Piano Concerto in F of 1925 is a far better piece than the *Rhapsody*, although there are still any number of passages that should have been rewritten or simply cut. But more than anything else, the Piano Concerto in F is about its glorious melodies, its syncopated rhythms, its percussive piano writing, and a singular and joyful energy that brilliantly represents New York in the 1920s. **Musical selection:** Gershwin, Piano Concerto in F, movement 3, rondo theme, first contrasting episode, and rondo theme restatement.

C. The *Concierto de Aranjuez* for Guitar and Orchestra (1939) of Joaquin Rodrigo (1901–1939) is the most popular guitar concerto ever written.

1. Although diphtheria left him blind at the age of three, Rodrigo became a successful composer. The *Concierto de Aranjuez* was composed in Paris in 1939 for the guitarist Regino Sainz de la Maza. The city of Aranjuez was a summer resort for Spanish nobility, and by naming his concerto for that city, Rodrigo evoked a certain stereotypical Spanish ambience: picturesque, innocent, and idealized, to stand in contrast with the contemporary horrors of the Spanish Civil War.
2. The concerto was premiered in Barcelona on November 9, 1940, and became an instant classic. It is cast in the usual three movements, fast–slow–fast. The middle movement, which Rodrigo said was a lament for those who died during the civil war, is the most famous. **Musical selection:** Rodrigo, *Concierto de Aranjuez* for Guitar and Orchestra, movement 2, opening.

D. Donald Erb (b. 1927), who began his musical career as a jazz trumpet player, has had a distinguished career as both a composer and a professor of composition.
1. His music is big, dramatic, and incredibly exciting. He has written 10 concerti, including the Trombone Concerto of 1976. This was commissioned by the trombonist Stuart Dempster and premiered on March 26, 1976, by the Saint Louis Symphony Orchestra under the baton of Leonard Slatkin.
2. In the finale, the soloist must employ a technique called *circular breathing*, in which he blows air into the instrument while inhaling through his nose. Dempster learned to do this by playing the Australian aboriginal *didgeridoo*. **Musical selection:** Erb, Trombone Concerto, movement 4 (in its entirety).

E. John Corigliano (b. 1938) is one of the outstanding composers of his generation and has written a tremendous amount of music in virtually every genre, including film scores. We will sample Corigliano's Oboe Concerto (1975), which is cast in five brief movements. The beginning of the first movement is one of the most sensational concerto openings in the repertoire. Entitled "Tuning Game," the concerto begins as if the orchestra were tuning up. It is not until about 20 seconds into the movement that we realize that the orchestra is not tuning up—the concerto has already begun! **Musical selection:** Corigliano, Oboe Concerto, movement 1, opening.

IV. Corigliano is the first name on our "composers-to-watch" list. Other composers whose careers we should keep an eye on are:

A. Christopher Rouse (b. 1949), who has written a number of concerti, of which his trombone concerto won the 1993 Pulitzer Prize in Music and a guitar concerto that won a Grammy in 2002.

B. Aaron Jay Kernis (b. 1960), another Pulitzer Prize winner; his English horn concerto, *Colored Field*, is superb.

C. Ellen Taafe Zwilich (b. 1939) is the first woman to win a Pulitzer Prize in Music. She composed a knockout trombone concerto in 1988.

D. Philip Glass (b. 1937) wrote an attractive violin concerto in 1987, which is, perhaps, his single best piece, its minimalist-inspired repetitions notwithstanding.

E. Jennifer Higdon (b. 1962) is most definitely a composer to watch. Her Concerto for Orchestra of 2002 picks up directly where Bartok's leaves off, and she has recently completed an oboe concerto.

V. Perhaps more than any other orchestral genre, the concerto grew directly out of vocal music and vocal compositional models.

A. Increasingly, the concerto, as a genre, became a metaphor for the individual voice, heard both in conflict and collaboration with the orchestra, itself a metaphor for the collective.

B. The concerto is a genuinely theatrical construct: Above and beyond its pitches and rhythms and forms, it is about the aspirations of the individual—us, as we venture forth and make our way in a sometimes hostile, sometimes friendly, but always challenging environment.

Timeline

c. 1600	Giovanni Gabrieli, *Buccinate in neomenia tuba*
c. 1680	Alessandro Stradella, Sonata in D Major for Trumpet and Strings
c. 1682	Georg Muffat, Concerto Grosso no. 5 in D Major
1690	Arcangelo Corelli, Concerto Grosso, op. 6, no. 8
c. 1695	Giuseppe Torelli, Concerto in D Major for Trumpet and Strings
c. 1715	Georg Philipp Telemann, Concerto in D Major for Three Corni di Caccia and Strings
c. 1715	Georg Philipp Telemann, Concerto in Bb Major for Strings
c. 1715	Georg Philipp Telemann, Triple Concerto in E Major for Flute, Oboe d'amore, and Viola d'amore
c. 1715	Georg Philipp Telemann, Oboe Concerto in F Minor
c. 1718	Francesco Manfredini, Concerto Grosso in C Major, op. 3, no. 12
c. 1718	Alessandro Marcello, Trumpet Concerto in C Minor
c. 1718	Johann Sebastian Bach, *Brandenburg* Concerto no. 3 in G Major
c. 1718	Johann Sebastian Bach, *Brandenburg* Concerto no. 6 in Bb Major
c. 1719	Johann Sebastian Bach, *Brandenburg* Concerto no. 1 in F major

c. 1719 .... Johann Sebastian Bach, *Brandenburg* Concerto no. 2 in F Major

c. 1719 .... Johann Sebastian Bach, *Brandenburg* Concerto no. 4 in G Major

c. 1721 .... Johann Sebastian Bach, *Brandenburg* Concerto no. 5 in D Major

c. 1721 .... Pietro Locatelli, Concerto Grosso in Bb Major, op. 1, no. 3

c. 1722 .... Tomaso Albinoni, Oboe Concerto in D Minor, op. 9, no. 2

pub. 1725 .... Antonio Vivaldi, Violin Concerto in E major, op. 8, no. 1, "Spring"

c. 1729 .... Antonio Vivaldi, Violin Concerto in Eb Major, op. 8, no. 5

pub. 1732 .... Francesco Geminiani, Concerto Grosso in E Minor, op. 3, no. 3

1739 .... George Frederick Handel, Concerto Grosso in Bb Major, op. 6, no. 7

c. 1755 .... Johann Joachim Quantz, Flute Concerto in D Major

c. 1755 .... Friedrich II of Prussia, Flute Concerto no. 3 in C Major

c. 1755 .... Giuseppe Tartini, Violin Concerto in A Major, D. 96

pub. 1770 .... Johann Christian Bach, Piano Concerto in Eb Major, op. 7, no. 5

1775 .... Wolfgang Mozart, Violin Concerto no. 4 in D Major, K. 218

1777 .... Wolfgang Mozart, Oboe Concerto in C Major, K. 271k

1778 .... Wolfgang Mozart, Flute Concerto in G major, K. 313

1778	Wolfgang Mozart, Concerto for Flute, Harp, and Orchestra in C Major, K. 299
1779	Wolfgang Mozart, Concerto for Two Pianos (or Harpsichords) and Orchestra in Eb Major, K. 365
1779	Wolfgang Mozart, Sinfonia Concertante in Eb Major for Violin, Viola, and Orchestra, K. 364
1786	Wolfgang Mozart, Horn Concerto in Eb Major, K. 495
1791	Wolfgang Mozart, Clarinet Concerto in A Major, K. 622
1796	Joseph Haydn, Trumpet Concerto in Eb Major
1803	Ludwig van Beethoven, Triple Concerto in C Major for Violin, 'Cello, and Piano, op. 56
1806	Ludwig van Beethoven, Piano Concerto no. 4 in G Major, op. 58
1819	Niccolo Paganini, Violin Concerto no. 1 in D Major
1819	Johann Hummel, Piano Concerto in B Minor, op. 89
1829	Frederic Chopin, Piano Concerto no. 2 in F Minor, op. 21
1831	Felix Mendelssohn, Piano Concerto in G Minor, op. 25
1836	Henry Vieuxtemps, Violin Concerto no. 2 in F# Minor, op. 19
1844	Felix Mendelssohn, Violin Concerto in E Minor, op. 64

1845	Robert Schumann, Piano Concerto in A Minor, op. 54
1850	Robert Schumann, 'Cello Concerto in A Minor, op. 129
1853	Franz Liszt, Piano Concerto no. 1 in Eb Major
1862	Henryk Wieniawski, Violin Concerto no. 2 in D Minor, op. 22
1869	Max Bruch, Violin Concerto no. 1 in G Minor, op. 26
1869	Edvard Grieg, Piano Concerto in A Minor, op. 16
1875	Peter Tchaikovsky, Piano Concerto no. 1 in Bb Minor, op. 23
1878	Peter Tchaikovsky, Violin Concerto in D Major, op. 35
1880	Peter Tchaikovsky, Piano Concerto no. 2 in G Major, op. 44
1881	Johannes Brahms, Piano Concerto no. 2 in Bb Major, op. 83
1883	Richard Strauss, Horn Concerto no. 1 in Eb Major, op. 11
1888	Ignaz Paderewski, Piano Concerto in A Minor, op. 17
1891	Sergei Rachmaninoff, Piano Concerto no. 1 in F# Minor, op. 1
1895	Antonin Dvorak, 'Cello Concerto in B Minor, op. 104
1898	Moritz Moszkowski, Piano Concerto in E Major, op. 59
1901	Sergei Rachmaninoff, Piano Concerto no. 2 in C Minor, op. 18

1904	Alexander Glazunov, Violin Concerto in A Minor, op. 82
1905	Jean Sibelius, Violin Concerto in D Minor, op. 47
1909	Sergei Rachmaninoff, Piano Concerto no. 3 in D Minor, op. 30
1911	Alexander Glazunov, Piano Concerto no. 1 in F Minor, op. 92
1912	Sergei Prokofiev, Piano Concerto no. 1 in Db Major, op. 10
1921	Sergei Prokofiev, Piano Concerto no. 3 in C Major, op. 26
1925	George Gershwin, Piano Concerto in F
1926	Aaron Copland, Piano Concerto
1928	Carl Nielsen, Clarinet Concerto, op. 57
1929	William Walton, Viola Concerto
1930	John Ireland, Piano Concerto in Eb Major
1931	Bela Bartok, Piano Concerto no. 2
1931	Maurice Ravel, Concerto in G Major
1931	Maurice Ravel, Piano Concerto in D Major for Left Hand
1933	Dmitri Shostakovich, Piano Concerto no. 1 in C Minor, op. 35
1934	Jacques Ibert, Flute Concerto
1935	Alban Berg, Violin Concerto
1935	Sergei Prokofiev, Violin Concerto no. 2 in G Minor, op. 63
1936	Aram Khachaturian, Piano Concerto in Db Major

1939	Joaquin Rodrigo, *Concierto de Aranjuez* for Guitar and Orchestra
1942	Arnold Schönberg, Piano Concerto, op. 42
1943	Bela Bartok, Concerto for Orchestra
1945	Richard Strauss, Oboe Concerto in D Major
1948	Dmitri Shostakovich, Violin Concerto no. 1 in A Minor, op. 77
1949	François Poulenc, Piano Concerto
1957	Dmitri Shostakovich, Piano Concerto no. 2 in F Major, op. 102
1959	Dmitri Shostakovich, 'Cello Concerto no. 1 in Eb Major
1961	Elliott Carter, Double Concerto for Harpsichord and Piano
1961	Alberto Ginastera, Piano Concerto no. 1, op. 28
1964	Dmitri Kabalevsky, 'Cello Concerto no. 2, op. 77
1970	Henri Dutilleux, 'Cello Concerto
1975	John Corigliano, Oboe Concerto
1976	Donald Erb, Trombone Concerto

Glossary

academy: Public concert in late 18th-, early 19th-century Vienna, Austria.

adagio: Slow.

allegretto (It.): Fast but not as fast as *allegro*.

allegro: (It.): Lively, somewhat fast.

andante (It.): Walking speed.

andantino (It.): Slower than walking speed.

aria: An air or song, though when used in the context of opera, a fairly sophisticated vocal number in which the musical elements provide the essential expressive message.

arpeggio (It.): Chord broken up into consecutively played notes.

augmented: (1) Major or perfect interval extended by a semitone, e.g., augmented sixth: C–A sharp. (2) Notes that are doubled in value; e.g., a quarter note becomes a half note. Augmentation is a device for heightening the drama of a musical section by extenuating the note values of the melody.

Baroque: Artistic style of the 16th and 17th centuries characterized by extreme elaboration. In music, the style was marked by the complex interplay of melodies, as manifest, for example, in a fugue.

basset clarinet: An instrument used extensively by the clarinetist Anton Stadler, pitched slightly lower than a standard clarinet.

bel canto (It.): Literally, "beautiful song," a style of both vocal and instrumental writing that celebrates beautiful melody.

bridge: Musical passage linking one section or theme to another. (See **transition**.)

BWV: Bach-Werke-Verseichnis, the catalog of the works of Johann Sebastian Bach.

cadence: Short harmonic formulas that close a musical section or movement. The most common formula is dominant–tonic (VI). (1) A *closed* (or *perfect*) *cadence* fully resolves: The dominant is followed by the expected tonic. (2) An *open* (or *imperfect*) *cadence* is a temporary point of rest, usually on an unresolved dominant. (3) A *deceptive* (or *interrupted*) *cadence* is one in which the dominant resolves to some chord other than the expected tonic.

cadenza: Passage for solo instrument in an orchestral work, usually a concerto, designed to showcase the player's skills.

chromatic: Scale in which all the pitches are present. On a keyboard, this translates as moving consecutively from white notes to black notes.

clarino: The upper range of a Baroque trumpet, as well as the Renaissance and Baroque designation for a trumpet.

Classical: Designation given to works of art of the 17th and 18th centuries, characterized by clear lines and balanced form.

coda: Section of music that brings a sonata-allegro movement to a close.

concertato/concertato principle: The use of multiple contrasting ensembles within an orchestra.

concertino: The group of soloists in a concerto grosso.

concertmaster: In early terminology, conductor; in modern terminology, the principal first violinist.

concerto grosso: An orchestral work that features multiple soloists grouped together into a coherent concertino.

consonance: Stable and resolved interval or chord; a state of musical rest.

counterpoint/contrapuntal: The simultaneous presentation of two or more melodic lines of equal importance.

crescendo (It.): Getting louder.

da capo (It.): Back to the top or beginning (instruction in a score).

development: Section in a classical sonata-allegro movement in which the main themes are developed.

diminished: Minor or perfect interval that is reduced by one semitone; e.g., minor seventh, C–B flat, becomes diminished when the minor is reduced by one semitone to become C sharp–B flat. Diminished sevenths are extremely unstable harmonies that can lead in a variety of harmonic directions.

dissonance: Unresolved and unstable interval or chord; a state of musical tension.

dominant: Fifth note of a scale and the key of that note; e.g., G is the dominant of C. The second theme in a classical sonata-allegro exposition first appears in the dominant.

double-exposition form: Sonata form adapted to the needs of a concerto.

double fugue: Complex fugue with two subjects, or themes.

drone: Note or notes, usually in the bass, sustained throughout a musical section or composition; characteristic of bagpipe music.

dynamics: Degrees of loudness, e.g., *piano* ("quiet") or *forte* ("loud"), indicated in a musical score.

Empfindsam (Ger.): Pre-Classical, mid-18th-century German musical style, characterized by melodic tunefulness, simplicity of utterance, and directness of expression.

enharmonic: Notes that are identical in sound but with different spellings depending on the key context, e.g., C sharp and D flat.

Enlightenment: Eighteenth-century philosophical movement characterized by rationalism and positing that individuals are responsible for their own destinies and that all men are born equal.

eroica (It.): Sobriquet, literally meaning "heroic" (given to Beethoven's Symphony no. 3).

exposition: The first large section of a fugue, in which the fugue subject is presented in each component voice, or the first large section of a sonata-form movement, during which the contrasting themes and key areas are presented.

fermata (It.): Pause.

flat: Note that has been lowered by one halftone in pitch; symbolized by "b."

forte (It.): Loud.

fortissimo (It.): Very loud.

French Overture: Invented by the French composer Jean-Baptiste Lully, court composer to King Louis XIV. The French overture was played at the theater to welcome the king and to set the mood for the action on stage. It is characterized by its grandiose themes; slow, stately tempo; dotted rhythms; and sweeping scales.

fugato (It.): Truncated fugue in which the exposition is not followed by true development.

fugue: Major, complex Baroque musical form, distantly related to the round, in which a theme (or subject) is repeated at different pitch levels in succession and is developed by means of various contrapuntal techniques.

Galant: Pre-Classical, mid-18th-century Italian musical style, characterized by melodic tunefulness, simplicity of utterance, and directness of expression.

Gesamtkunstwerk (Ger.): All-inclusive artwork or art form, containing music, drama, poetry, dance, and so on; term coined by Richard Wagner.

frandioso (It.): Grandly, majestically.

Heiligenstadt Testament: Confessional document penned by Beethoven at a time of extreme psychological crisis. In it, he despairs over his realization that he is going deaf but determines to soldier on.

hemiola: Temporary use of a displaced accent to produce a feeling of changed meter. Beethoven uses it to effect an apparent change from triple (3/4) meter to duple (2/4) meter, without actually changing the meter.

home key: Main key of a movement or composition.

homophonic: Musical passage or piece in which there is one main melody and everything else is accompaniment.

interval: Distance in pitch between two tones, e.g., C–G (upwards), a fifth.

inversion: Loosely applied to indicate a reversal in direction; e.g., a melody that goes up, goes down in inversion and vice versa. Its strict definitions are as follows: (1) *Harmonic inversion*: The bottom note of an interval, or chord, is transferred to its higher octave, or its higher note is transferred to its lower octave; e.g., C–E–G (played together) becomes E–G–C or E–C–G. (2) *Melodic inversion*: An ascending interval (one note played after the other) is changed to its corresponding descending interval and vice versa; e.g., C–D–E becomes C–B–A.

K. numbers: Koechel numbers, named after L. von Koechel, are a cataloging identification attached to works by Mozart.

Kapellmeister (Ger.): Orchestra director/composer.

key: Central tonality, named after the main note of that tonality.

keyed trumpet: An instrument invented by the trumpeter Anton Weidinger in 1793.

larghetto (It.): Slowly.

largo (It.): Broad, slow.

maestro di cappela (It.): Music director of a church or municipality; the Italian equivalent of the German *Kapellmeister*.

major/minor key system: Two essential *modes*, or pitch palettes, of European tonal music; *major* is generally perceived as being the brighter sounding of the two, and *minor*, the darker sounding of the two.

Mannheim School: Composers, orchestra, and teaching institutions of the court of Mannheim between 1741 and 1778.

measure (abbr. ms.): Metric unit; space between two bar lines.

melisma: Tightly wound, elaborate melodic line.

meter: Rhythmic measure, e.g., triple meter (3/4), in which there are three beats to the bar, or duple meter (2/4), in which there are two beats to the bar.

metric modulation: Main beat remains the same while the rhythmic subdivisions change. This alters the meter without disturbing the tempo.

minuet: A graceful and dignified dance of the 17th and 18th centuries, played in moderately slow three-quarter time.

minuet and trio: Form of a movement (usually the third) in a classical symphony. The movement is in ternary (ABA) form, with the first minuet repeated after the trio and each section itself repeated.

modal ambiguity: Harmonic ambiguity, in which the main key is not clearly identified.

mode: Major or minor key (in modern Western usage).

modulation: Change from one key to another.

molto sostenuto (It.): Very sustained.

motive: Short musical phrase that can be used as a building block in compositional development.

movement: Independent section within a larger work.

musette: (1) Bagpipe common in Europe in the 17th and 18th centuries. (2) Piece of music in rustic style with a drone bass.

musical form: Overall formulaic structure of a composition, e.g., sonata form; also the smaller divisions of the overall structure, such as the development section.

nationalism: Incorporation of folk or folk-like music into concert works and operas.

oboe d'amore: An alto oboe, pitched a minor third below a standard oboe.

opus: Work, as in a musical work or composition.

ostinato (It.): Motive that is repeated over and over again.

overture: Music that precedes an opera or play.

pastorale: A musical work that evokes the countryside.

pedal note: Pitch sustained for a long period of time against which other changing material is played. A pedal harmony is a sustained chord serving the same purpose.

pianissimo (It.): Very quiet.

piano (It.): Soft or quiet.

piano trio: Composition for piano, violin, and 'cello.

pivot modulation: A tone common to two chords is used to effect a smooth change of key. For example, F sharp–A–C sharp (F sharp-minor triad) and F–A–C (F-major triad) have A in common. This note can serve as a pivot to swing the mode from F sharp minor to F major.

pizzicato (It.): Very short (plucked) notes.

polyphony: Dominant compositional style of the pre-Classical era, in which multiple melodies are played together (linear development), as opposed to one melody played with harmonic accompaniment.

polyrhythm: Simultaneous use of contrasting rhythms.

polytonality: Simultaneous use of two or more different keys (major and/or minor) or modes.

presto (It.): Fast.

quartet: (1) Ensemble of four instruments. (2) Piece for four instruments.

recapitulation: Section following the development in a sonata-allegro movement, in which the main themes return in their original form.

recitative: Operatic convention in which the lines are half-sung, half-spoken.

retrograde: Backwards.

retrograde inversion: Backwards and upside down.

ripieno (It.): Passage played by the whole orchestra, as opposed to a passage played by solo instruments (*concertante*).

ripieno concerto (It.): A concerto with no clearly defined solo part(s) above and beyond the first violin part.

ritardando (It.): Gradually getting slower (abbreviation: *ritard*).

ritornello (It.): Refrain.

Romanticism: Nineteenth-century artistic movement that stressed emotion over intellect and celebrated the boundlessness, the fantastic, and the extremes of experience.

rondo (It.): Musical form in which a principal theme returns like a refrain after various contrasting episodes.

rubato (It.): Extreme flexibility in approach to tempo.

Russian Five: A group of five mid-19th-century Russian composers (Balakirev, Cui, Mussorgky, Rimsky-Korsakov, and Borodin) dedicated to creating a Russian concert music based on the Russian language and Russian folk music.

scherzando (It.): In a joking manner.

scherzo (It.): Name given by Beethoven and his successors to designate a whimsical, often witty, fast movement in triple time.

semitone: Smallest interval in Western music; on the keyboard, the distance between a black note and a white note; also, B–C and E–F.

sequence: Successive repetitions of a motive at different pitches. A compositional technique for extending melodic ideas.

sextuplets: A group of six notes.

sharp: Note that has been raised one halftone in pitch; symbolized by #.

sonata-allegro form (also known as *sonata form*): Most important musical structure of the Classical era. It is based on the concept of dramatic interaction between two contrasting themes and structured in four parts, sometimes with an introduction to the exposition, or first part. The exposition introduces the main themes that will be developed in the development section. The themes return in the recapitulation section, and the movement is closed with a coda.

stringendo (It.): Compressing time; getting faster.

string quartet: (1) Ensemble of four stringed instruments: two violins, viola, and 'cello. (2) Composition for such an ensemble.

Sturm und Drang (Ger.): "Storm and stress"; late-18th-century literary movement.

symphonic poem: One-movement orchestral composition depicting a story and usually based on literature.

symphony: Large-scale instrumental composition for orchestra, containing several movements. The Viennese Classical symphony usually had four movements.

syncopation: Displacement of the expected accent from a strong beat to a weak beat and vice versa.

theme and variations: Musical form in which a theme is introduced, then treated to a series of variations on some aspect of that theme.

tone poem: See **Symphonic poem**.

tonic: First note of the scale; main key of a composition or musical section.

transition (or **bridge**): Musical passage linking two sections.

tremolo (It.): A rapid back-and-forth oscillation between two different pitches.

triad: Chord consisting of three notes: the root, the third, and the fifth, e.g., C–E–G, the triad of C major.

trill: A rapid back-and-forth oscillation between two adjacent pitches.

trio: (1) Ensemble of three instruments. (2) Composition for three instruments. (3) Type of minuet, frequently rustic in nature and paired with another minuet to form a movement in a Classical-era symphony.

triplet: Three notes occurring in the space of one beat.

tritone: Interval of six semitones that produces an extreme dissonance and begs for immediate resolution.

tutti (It.): The whole orchestra plays together.

Viennese Classical style: Style that dominated European music in the late 18th century. It is characterized by clarity of melodies, harmonies, and rhythms and balanced, proportional musical structures.

viole d'amore: A viola-like instrument of the viol family.

voice: A pitch or register, commonly used to refer to the four melodic pitches: soprano, alto, tenor, and bass.

Featured Composers

Baroque Era:

Giovanni Gabrieli (c. 1555–1612)

Alessandro Stradella (1644–1682)

Arcangelo Corelli (1653–1713)

Georg Muffat (1653–1704)

Giuseppe Torelli (1658–1709)

Tomaso Albinoni (1671–1751)

Antonio Vivaldi (1678–1741)

Georg Philipp Telemann (1681–1767)

Alessandro Marcello (1684–1750)

Francesco Manfredini (1684–1762)

Johann Sebastian Bach (1685–1750)

George Frederick Handel (1685–1759)

Francesco Geminiani (1687–1762)

Pietro Locatelli (1695–1764)

Classical Era:

Giuseppe Tartini (1692–1770)

Johann Joachim Quantz (1697–1773)

Frederick II ("the Great") of Prussia (1712–1786)

Joseph Haydn (1732–1809)

Johann Christian Bach (1735–1782)

Wolfgang Mozart (1756–1791)

Ludwig van Beethoven (1770–1827)

Romantic Era:

Johann Nepomuk Hummel (1778–1837)

Niccolo Paganini (1782–1840)

Felix Mendelssohn (1809–1847)

Frederic Chopin (1810–1849)

Robert Schumann (1810–1856)

Franz Liszt (1811–1886)
Henry Vieuxtemps (1820–1881)
Johannes Brahms (1833–1897)
Henryk Wieniawski (1835–1880)
Max Bruch (1838–1920)
Peter Tchaikovsky (1840–1893)
Antonin Dvorak (1841–1904)
Edvard Grieg (1843–1907)
Moritz Moszkowski (1854–1925)
Ignaz Paderewski (1860–1941)
Richard Strauss (1864–1949)
Sergei Rachmaninoff (1873–1943)

20th Century:

Alexander Glazunov (1865–1936)
Carl Nielsen (1865–1931)
Jean Sibelius (1865–1957)
Arnold Schönberg (1874–1951)
Maurice Ravel (1875–1937)
John Ireland (1879–1962)
Bela Bartok (1881–1945)
Alban Berg (1885–1935)
Jacques Ibert (1890–1962)
Sergei Prokofiev (1891–1953)
George Gershwin (1898–1937)
François Poulenc (1899–1963)
Aaron Copland (1900–1990)
Joaquin Rodrigo (1901–1999)
William Walton (1902–1983)
Aram Khachaturian (1903–1978)
Dmitri Kabalevsky (1904–1987)
Dmitri Shostakovich (1906–1975)

Elliott Carter (born 1908)
Henri Dutilleux (born 1916)
Alberto Ginastera (1916–1983)
Donald Erb (born 1927)
John Corigliano (born 1938)

Bibliography

Essential Reading:

Layton, Robert ed. *A Companion to the Concerto*. New York: Schirmer Books, 1988. A compendium of excellent articles spanning the history of the concerto from its inception through the late 20th century. The appendices include a recommended discography, the selections with which I agree enthusiastically.

Roeder, Michael Thomas. *A History of the Concerto*. Portland, OR: Amadeus Press, 1994. The Roeder is exactly what its title claims it is: a comprehensive, chronological history of the concerto, by far the best such source available. It is not the sort of book that one reads from cover to cover, but rather, like any encyclopedic source, it is an informational source that can be mined at one's leisure.

Steinberg, Michael. *The Concerto: A Listener's Guide*. Oxford: Oxford University Press, 1998. Michael Steinberg is one of the most brilliant writers on music of our time. The entries—arranged alphabetically by composer—are fleshed-out versions of program notes Steinberg created over the years for the Boston Symphony Orchestra, the San Francisco Symphony, and the New York Philharmonic. Always entertaining and insightful, Steinberg's notes are relatively brief but packed with information.

Supplementary Reading:

Adey, Christopher. *Orchestral Performance: A Guide for Conductors and Players*. London: Faber & Faber, 1998.

Ashman, Mike. *Richard Strauss—Wind Concertos*. CD note; Teldec 3984-23913-2, 2001.

Boyden, John. *Stick to the Music*. London: Souvenir Press, 1984.

Bukofzer, Manfred E. *Music in the Baroque Era*. New York: W.W. Norton, 1947.

Carrell, Norman. *Bach's Brandenburg Concerti*. London: George Allen & Unwin, Ltd., 1963.

Clapham, John. *Dvorak*. London: David and Charles, 1979.

Clarke, Sedgwick. *Rachmaninoff Piano Concerto no. 1*. CD note; Mercury 434 333-2.

Corigliano, John. *Oboe Concerto*. CD note; RCA 60395-2-RG.

Creative Quotations. www.creativequotations.com/one/1850.htm.

Dabul, Elena. "Alberto Ginastera on the *Fundacion Ostinato*." members.tripod.com/~ostinato/ginasbio.html.

Downes, Edward. *Guide to Symphonic Music*. New York: Walker and Company, 1981.

Erb, Donald. *Trombone Concerto*. CD note; Koss KC-3302.

Everett, Paul. *Vivaldi: The Four Seasons and Other Concertos, op. 8*. Cambridge: Cambridge University Press, 1996.

Fay, Laurel E. *Shostakovich: A Life*. Oxford: Oxford University Press, 2000.

Geiringer, Karl. *Brahms: His Life and Work*. Boston and New York: Houghton Mifflin Company, 1936.

Girdlestone, Cuthbert. *Mozart and His Piano* Concertos. New York: Dover, 1964.

Gould, Glenn. *Arnold Schoenberg: A Perspective*. Cincinnati: University of Cincinnati Press, 1964.

Grayson, David. *Mozart: Piano Concertos no. 20 in D Minor, K. 466, and no. 21 in C major, K. 467*. Cambridge: Cambridge University Press, 1998.

Grout, Donald, and Claude Palisca. *A History of Western Music*, 4th ed. New York: W.W. Norton, 1988.

Halbreich, Harry. *François Poulenc, Concerto for Piano*. CD note; Erato ECD 88140.

Holden, Anthony. *Tchaikovsky: A Biography*. New York: Random House, 1995.

Hopkins, Antony. *Talking about Music*. London: Pan Books, 1977.

Hughes, Robert. *Goya*. New York: Knopf, 2003.

Hutchings, Arthur. *The Baroque Concerto*, rev. ed. New York: Charles Scribner's Sons, 1979.

Jameson, Michael. *Henri Dutilleux, 'Cello Concerto*. CD note; EMI 7243 5 67868 2.

Johnson, Stephen. *Sergei Prokofiev Violin Concertos*. CD note; Virgin 7 90734-2, 1988.

Kenyon, Nicholas, ed. *The BBC Proms Pocket Guide to Great Concertos*. London: Faber & Faber, 2003.

King, A. Hyatt. *Mozart Wind and String Concertos*. Seattle: University of Washington Press, 1978.

Lawson, Colin. *Mozart—Clarinet Concerto*. Cambridge: Cambridge University Press, 1996.

Lebrecht, Norman. *The Book of Musical Anecdotes*. New York: Free Press, 1985.

———. *The Maestro Myth*, revised and updated. New York: Citadel Press, 2001.

Leinsdorf, Erich. *The Composer's Advocate: A Radical Orthodoxy for Musicians*. New Haven, CT: Yale University Press, 1981.

Marshall, Robert L. *Mozart Speaks*. New York: Schirmer Books, 1991.

Meikle, Robert. *Flötenkonzerte aus Sanssouci*. CD booklet, DG D 108081.

Morrison, Bryce. *Hummel, Piano Concerto in B Minor, op. 89*. CD booklet, Chandos 8507.

Nelson, Wendell. *The Concerto*. Dubuque, IA: Wm. C. Brown, 1969.

Nicholas, Jeremy. *Paderewski and Moszkowski Piano Concertos*. CD note; Hyperion CDA66452.

Norris, Geoffrey. *Rakhmaninov*. London: J. M. Dent & Sons, 1976.

Norris, Jeremy. *The Russian Piano Concerto*. Vol. 1: *The Nineteenth Century*. Bloomington and Indianapolis: Indiana University Press, 1994.

Orga, Ates. *Khachaturian Piano Concerto in Db*. CD note; Sanctuary CD 43625 30372.

———. *Tchaikovsky Piano Concerto no. 2*. CD note; Naxos 8.550820.

Palisca, Claude. *Baroque Music*. Englewood Cliffs, NJ: Prentice-Hall, 1968.

Palmer, Christopher. *Walton Concerto for Viola and Orchestra*. CD note; Chandos CHAN 9106.

Pellegrino, Charles. *Ghosts of Vesuvius*. New York: William Morrow, 2004.

Penesco, Anne. *Giuseppe Tartini—Three Concerti for Violin*. CD Note; Erato CD 2292-45380-2, 1985.

Plantinga, Leon. *Beethoven's Concertos*. New York: W.W. Norton, 1999.

Quantz, J. J. *On Playing the Flute*, 2nd ed. Boston: Northeastern University Press, 2001.

Rink, John. *Chopin: The Piano Concertos*. Cambridge: Cambridge University Press, 1997.

Rosen, Charles. *Arnold Schoenberg*. Princeton, NJ: Princeton University Press, 1975.

Sadie, Stanley, ed. *New Grove Dictionary of Music and Musicians*. New York: Macmillan, 1980.

Schiff, David. *The Music of Elliott Carter*, new ed. London: Faber & Faber, 1998.

Schonberg, Harold. *Lives of the Great Composers*, 3rd ed. New York: Simon and Schuster, 1997.

———. *Fundamentals of Musical Composition*. London and Northampton: Faber & Faber, 1967.

———. *The Great Pianists*. New York: Simon and Schuster, 1987.

Shostakovich, Dmitri, and Solomon Volkov. *Testimony: The Memoirs of Dmitri Shostakovich*. New York: Harper and Row, 1979.

Slonimsky, Nicholas. *Lexicon of Musical Invective*. Seattle: University of Washington Press, 1975.

Solomon, Maynard. *Mozart: A Life*. New York: Harper Collins, 1995.

Steiner, George. *Tolstoy or Dostoevsky*. New York: Vintage, 1961.

Stevens, Halsey. *The Life and Music of Bela Bartok*, revised ed. Oxford and New York: Oxford University Press, 1967.

Stravinsky, Igor, and Robert Craft. *Memories and Commentaries*. Berkeley and Los Angeles: University of California Press, 1959/1981.

Svejda, Jim. *Copland: Piano Concerto*. CD note; Delos DE 3154.

Swafford, Jan. *Johannes Brahms: A Biography*. New York: Alfred A. Knopf, 1997.

Tovey, Donald Francis. *Essays in Musical Analysis*. Vol. 3. London: Oxford University Press, 1937.

Walker, Alan. *Franz Liszt*. Vol. 1: *The Virtuoso Years (1811–1847)*. New York: Knopf, 1983.

———. *Franz Liszt*. Vol. 3: *The Final Years (1861–1886)*. Ithaca, NY: Cornell University Press, 1996.

———, ed. *Robert Schumann: The Man and His Music*. London: Faber & Faber, 1976.

Warrack, John. *Tchaikovsky*. New York: Scribners, 1973.

Weiss, Piero, and Richard Taruskin. *Music in the Western World: A History in Documents*. New York: Schirmer Books, 1984.

Whittal, Arnold. *Berg/Schönberg Violin Concertos and Piano Concerto*. CD note; Universal B0001741-02.

Zaslaw, Neal, and William Cowdery. *The Complete Mozart*. New York: W.W. Norton, 1990.

Notes

Notes

Notes